ONE Small *yes*

## Advance Praise

"Not sure I've ever met a person more focused and passionate about serving and enriching lives of others. When Misty speaks people listen, when she writes people read. She's a difference maker."

—**Dave Skogen**, Chairman Festival Foods

"Misty Lown is a leader of consequence. She knows how to build a winning business through authenticity, grit and determination. Is her book a must-read? YES!"

—**Bill McDermott**, Entrepreneur, CEO, Bestselling Author of *Winners Dream*

"If you want to build a life and a business that makes a difference, Misty Lown will show you the way. What she has accomplished one "yes" at a time is an inspiration to entrepreneurs everywhere. If you want to be inspired as you learn new ways to live a life of significance then *One Small Yes* is for you."

—**Darren Hardy**, *New York Times* Bestselling Author of *The Compound Effect* and former Publisher and Founding Editor, *SUCCESS* Magazine

"This is a book that should have been written years ago, but better late than never! Misty is a brilliant business owner, who understands the experience is key. She is literally the Steve Jobs of the dance world, and the steps she's taken to build her business apply to any business owner out there."

—**Cody Foster**, CEO, Advisors Excel

"In my world it's all about getting things done now—tomorrow is full of a whole new set of challenges. Misty Lown leads the way as an exemplary example of "doers". I've watched Misty grow from one small business to global influence in the span of a few years. *One Small Yes* is not just her story, it's for every leader who wants to stop dreaming and start doing."

—**Marc A. Sparks**, Chairman, CEO, Timber Creek Capital, LLC

"I've been in business for over forty years and in that time I've never met someone quite like Misty Lown. Misty has raised the bar for achievement for leaders everywhere, including me. The business lessons she shares are life lessons that can help anyone move their ideas forward. One Small Yes is a practical template for making a difference no matter what type of business you are in."

—**Dave Liniger**, CEO, RE/MAX

"*One Small Yes* was written for people who want to make an impact! It isn't just about saying yes or replicating another success story. Misty Lown gives you a peek into her personal journey towards success and offers practical advice on finding your yes. If you have a dream but don't know where to start, this book will help you embrace challenges and lead you through the small yes's (and sometimes no's) towards your own success and happiness."

—**Honorée Corder**, Bestselling Author of *Vision to Reality*

"I've been in the business of building businesses my entire life and I've never experienced the WOW factor quite like Misty Lown delivers. She has done more with her small business in twenty years than most people do in a lifetime. Misty shares the story of how she did it in *One Small Yes*, but it's much more than that—it's a way for readers to find and follow their own unique callings. If you want to achieve big results and how to WOW others with your business, start here."

—**Paul Niccum**, CEO of Paradise Capital, Author of *No Regrets: How to Exit Your Privately Held Business*

"Misty Lown delivers the goods. *One Small Yes* serves up a treasure chest of real strategies on how to achieve BIG results in your business and life. I have watched Misty in action for years and you will benefit greatly from her wisdom and heart."

—**Todd Duncan**, Founder/CEO, The Duncan Group

"*One Small Yes* taught me how to stop with the busy work and connect with my life's work. It's the perfect pick-me-up for every entrepreneur. Misty is an entrepreneur with heart, someone who genuinely cares for the success of others."

—**Austin Roberson**, Founder, StudioOwnersAcademy.com

"Misty Lown writes in an engaging, authentic manner about how to pursue your calling and succeed in business. She shares lessons from her own pursuit of calling to open a dance studio despite formidable challenges. She went on to develop a training program that now positively influences 60,000 kids a week one small yes at a time. She is making a difference and her story will inspire readers to do likewise."

—**Richard (Rick) J. Goossen**, PhD,
Chairman, Entrepreneurial Leaders Organization

"No matter your season or station in life, you will find *One Small Yes* a fast paced and informative road map to find and pursue your calling. Misty Lown weaves her personal experience and the wisdom of other leaders on a journey toward purpose. Lown's authenticity is revealed in her stories of everyday life as a teacher and entrepreneur. The book is both inspirational and practical. Say "Yes" to this compelling and practical guide to a more fulfilling life."

—**Richard B. Artman**, PhD, President, Viterbo University

"*One Small Yes* is yet another brilliant gift to the world from Misty Lown. It is an essential read for anyone, whether they are well on their path, or seeking to find it. It shows how a regular girl became an extraordinary woman *One Small Yes* at a time. I was inspired by Misty from the moment I met her, and I was fascinated with how one woman could own so many businesses, have 5 children, travel the world inspiring others and remain such a down-to-earth, beautiful human being. Her humble and often vulnerable account of how she made the journey will open the gateway for so many others."

—**Lisa Howell**, (B.Phty), Registered Physiotherapist, Founder and Owner of Perfect Form Physiotherapy and The Ballet Blog

"Every person has a story and Misty Lown is using hers to help others make a difference with theirs. If you have a desire to use your gifts and talents to have a positive impact on lives of your clients and the community you live in, *One Small Yes* is a must-read. Misty has helped to change the lives of tens of thousands of people and will show practical tools to make your positive mark in the world as well!"

—**Kindra Hall**, *Strategic Storytelling Consultant*

"*One Small Yes* shows you how the life and business you want can be yours, when you simply decide. Misty's journey is not only inspiring, it demonstrates that by taking small steps each and every day that we can really achieve anything. It's a must read for anyone who's at a point in their life when they know they could be achieving more, from impacting the lives of more people to filling up their own cup to achieve more fulfillment. This book guides you through a story of hope, hard work and heart with plenty of actionable takeaways that you can apply to your business and life so you too can achieve your very own version of success!"

—**Clint Salter**, CEO, Dance Studio Owners Association

"If you've ever had a dream but thought you lost it, if you've ever stopped trying because the road seemed impossible, or if you've ever just flat-out given up, this book will restore your hope. *One Small Yes* doesn't just tell the story of an impossible dream coming true for Misty Lown–it gives you the exact steps she took to make it a reality."

—**Amy Anderson**, Founder YouCanFreelance.com
and former Senior Editor of *SUCCESS* Magazine

"Misty Lown is first class and this book will help you and your business get to the front of the line! As the owner of several small businesses with over 30 years of experience I recommend you take the time to read this informative book"

—**Steve Sirico**, Founder Dance Teacher Web
& D'Valda and Sirico Dance and Music Centre

"Misty is an architect for success… She is allowing us to walk with her thru the blueprints of our dreams and see if our structure has a solid foundation. *One Small Yes* is a game changer for anyone wanting to have a lifetime of success."

—**Michelle Brogan**, Founder, Dance Revolution
and Epicenter for the Arts

"I constantly challenge myself and others to create meaning in our lives by discovering what is our passion and purpose. Once we learn that important truth we are then compelled to use our God-given gifts to make meaningful impact, honouring our Creator by becoming the brightest and best version of ourselves. Misty Lown is quite literally one of the most incredible examples of someone who lives life to its fullest; striving to become a shining beacon of hope for others. I believe that if you study the ideas shared in this book and put them into practice, that you will find it transformational to your life."

—**Brad Pederson**, CEO, Tech4Kids

# ONE
## Small *yes*

### Small Decisions that
### Lead to BIG Results

## MISTY LOWN

NEW YORK

NASHVILLE • MELBOURNE • VANCOUVER

# ONE Small *yes*
## Small Decisions that Lead to BIG Results

Published in New York, New York, by Morgan James Publishing in partnership with Difference Press. Morgan James is a trademark of Morgan James, LLC. www.MorganJamesPublishing.com

The Morgan James Speakers Group can bring authors to your live event. For more information or to book an event visit The Morgan James Speakers Group at www.TheMorganJamesSpeakersGroup.com.

Any perceived slight of any individual or organization is purely unintentional.

Any resemblance, within this book, to real persons living or dead is purely coincidental apart from my own stories that are true to the author.

ISBN 978-1-68350-270-8 paperback
ISBN 978-1-68350-271-5 eBook
ISBN 978-1-68350-272-2 hardcover
Library of Congress Control Number:
2016916267

**Cover Design by:**
Heidi Miller

**Interior Design by:**
Bonnie Bushman
The Whole Caboodle Graphic Design

**Editing:**
Cynthia Kane

**Author's photo courtesy of:**
Megan McCluskey

In an effort to support local communities, raise awareness and funds, Morgan James Publishing donates a percentage of all book sales for the life of each book to Habitat for Humanity Peninsula and Greater Williamsburg.

Get involved today! Visit
www.MorganJamesBuilds.com

# Dedication

**To Mitch:**

From the first time I saw you in math class I knew you were the one. Twenty-five years, five children and several minivans later, you're still the one to make me smile. I love the way you dive all-in to teach the kids. If it's skiing, you are driving the boat; if it's snowboarding, you are on the hill. I love that you teach by example in all ways—especially in how you serve others. When I watch you build things in the garage with the kids it makes me want to freeze time. It's going so fast! I am blessed to do life with you and proud to be your wife.

**To Isabella:**

What a joy it has been to see you blossom into a confident young woman. Even though you are almost ready to drive, you'll always be my one-in-million Snugpie! I am in awe of how hard you work at everything you do. Your joy for dance and school is contagious. But most importantly, you are a young woman of kindness and compassion. Watching you care for your friends and Stella makes my heart squeeze. I can't wait to see what kind of calling God puts on your heart as you move through high school and beyond. Keep pressing into the heart of Jesus, Isabella. He'll never let you down.

### To Mason:

I can hardly believe that little boy I brought home from the hospital during a snowstorm is now a teenager. Mason, God has given you some amazing gifts! You are the funniest kid I know and smart-as-a-whip to boot. The way you can remember facts about history and games has always amazed me, but the thing I love most about you is your sweet spirit. You are always the first one to ask how my day is when I get home and the first to give your aunt and grandma a hug. Your Grandpa Glen would be so proud of all of your accomplishments. I know we are. Keep God first place in your life; he has a great calling that is just for you!

### To Sam:

Sammer! How can it be that you just graduated from elementary school and will be going to middle school next year? I swear I was just walking you to the bus stop for pre-school and watching you chase snowflakes. Now you are a true Renaissance man in the making. You excel at sports and have added cooking class and dance conventions to your lineup of things you do really well. You are the king of wrestling matches and a never-ending source of creativity in art and writing. Your dad and I know that if we can't find you, you are off exploring your love of reading somewhere. Sam, I can't wait to see what God will call you to in this world—it's going to be great!

**To Max:**

I can't believe that the little boy who loved to play Thomas the Train in his room so much is now big enough to spend hours playing basketball outside with the neighborhood kids–and I do mean hours! Max, I have taught students your age for 25 years and I've never met anybody with more focus and diligence than you. Whatever you do, you are all in. I love that about you, Buddy! Even though you are only nine, your dad and I can already see that God has planted some pretty cool dreams in your heart about sports. Get ready, Golden State! But mostly, I love how you always want to honor God. Never lose that–guard it like a treasure in your heart.

**To Benji:**

Benji, you are my little buddy. You have the sweetest heart, the wildest dance moves and a blue blanket for a best friend. When your sister was born, I celebrated all the "firsts" and now I am cherishing every one of the "last" moments with you. Just a couple of weeks ago it was the last time your dad and I would have a child graduate from first grade. You are officially one of the big boys now! You have quite a gift for soccer and fishing. We love watching you score goals and catch the big ones on your own. You are big in all you do! Never lose your heart for worship. God loves to hear you sing, Benji!

PS. My offer for you to stay seven forever still stands.

*And to God, who holds all things together and is the Author of Life.*

# Table of Contents

# Introduction

Every great story begins with one small yes. I love to watch documentaries and read biographies of thought leaders and entrepreneurs. The backstory of a person's career lends insight into his or her motivations and sheds light on the challenges encountered while building brands, businesses and bold missions. Regardless of a person's eventual claim to fame, or even starting point, one theme runs steady through my fascination with a change maker's journey…and that is the theme of "one small yes."

Every hero you've seen on the screen of a docudrama or have read about in the pages of a book has had to make one small yes choice of some kind–probably many. It could have been a yes to start a business despite a lack of resources or ability, a yes to keep going against incredible odds or a yes to get up after falling down. Sometimes, it was the tiniest of all yeses–simply showing up one more time–that made the difference between going the distance with an idea–or going home empty handed. My favorite yes moments of a person's story have always been the unconventional ones–the times when people zigged when you expected them to zag and they not only landed on their feet, they landed ahead of the pack!

My fascination with one small yes stories comes naturally to me. Some of my earliest memories involved watching my parents raise their hands first to say yes to help someone in need. Someone sick? Mom's goulash was on their doorstep. House fire? No problem, you can have some of our things. And when a family friend was seriously burned in a gas range explosion, my mom said yes to turning our living room into a recovery unit for four months to span the time between hospital care and when our friend could function on his own.

My dad was no different in his yes disposition; he just had different ways of going about it. Fixing things, lending tools and climbing ladders was my dad's strong suit. I've always joked that the TV character MacGyver had nothing on my dad's ability to figure things out. If a strong arm or a smart eye on a project was what you needed, my dad was your guy. Remember the farm crisis of the 1980s? Dad was saying yes to organize semi-loads of hay for farm aid before Willie Nelson made it a concert series. The word yes was in his blood.

My parents' natural inclination to say yes to the good stuff was important in my development, but their willingness to keep saying yes to the game of life when things were *not good* was crucial. In the face of job loss, financial challenges, divorce and even personal struggles, giving up was never an option. They just kept doing what they always did: showing my sister and me how to figure out life one small yes at a time.

Looking back, one memory rises above the rest. I was a middle school student hiding in the living room in order to listen to a conversation my parents were having around the kitchen table.

My dad, age 40 at the time, had lost his job as a top driver at the trucking company where he had worked for most of my childhood.

Although this was a life-altering circumstance for our family, there was no drama about the situation. My dad simply stated in a matter-of-fact voice that he would go dig ditches for the railroad to provide for the family.

And he did. After he said "yes" to the ditches, he said yes to going to signal school and learning a new trade. When that wasn't enough to keep things going, my mom said yes to a night job as a bartender to make ends meet. Then she said yes to cleaning houses. And when their divorce was final, they said yes to working together to raise my sister and me despite their differences.

My parents' ability to say yes to the daily challenges they faced hard-wired a default to the small yes in my own DNA. And their willingness to say yes to the unconventional–like letting me take the city bus to dance class across town and a taxi home when we didn't have a car–developed in me a perseverance in life and dance that still serves me today.

My dad's figure-it-out attitude combined with my mom's faith had a profound impact on my view of what is possible in life. How else could it be that a kid born with a clubfoot, who spent part of her teen years making poor choices, would end up owning a dance studio and positively influencing tens of thousands of kids, if not for the grace of God and a pile of perseverance?

The path I took to owning a business that makes a difference in the lives of many has been an unlikely and winding thread of unusual yeses to say the least:

- Saying yes to the challenge of dancing with a recovered clubfoot and markedly unequal leg lengths.
- Saying yes to teaching daily dance classes in my hometown during high school, instead of taking a traditional high school job, in order to pay for more lessons.

- Saying the tiniest yes, despite being scared out of my mind, to audition for a training program at the world famous Alvin Ailey American Dance Center in New York City.
- Saying an unconventional yes to opening a dance studio instead of taking a place in the Alvin Ailey training program after college.

As I write this book, one leg is still shorter than the other and my feet still turn out unequally. Even so, I am running a dance studio that serves more than 750 students per year and a licensed affiliation program of 164 dance studios in the U.S., Canada, Australia, Aruba and Dubai that serves more than 60,000 students each week. I've launched an online dance magazine that receives hundreds of thousands of visits a month from teenagers, along with a dance competition and a dancewear store. My husband and I also own self-storage units and a property development company. When you add five amazing, energetic children into the mix it's easy to understand why the question I am asked most often as I travel the world speaking and teaching is "How do you do it?"

The frequency of this question used to puzzle me because the answer is so simple. How do I do it? One small yes at a time. Yes to my calling of teaching kids, yes to faith, yes to showing up daily in business, yes to pruning and prioritizing my work, yes to the tiniest progress on the hardest days, yes to unconventional wisdom and yes to saying no at the right time.

You see I don't actually DO "it." I simply say yes to all the pieces that MAKE "it"—one small yes at a time. The truth of the matter is that if I thought of the enormity of what I have going on and the improbable ideas that I still have in front of me, or even just the task of making dinner while getting the kids to their evening activities, I wouldn't even know how to begin to tackle THAT. But a small yes to the next thing that needs to be done? Now THAT is possible.

No, I don't DO "it" at all. Not even by a long shot. I have simply discovered how to navigate life with grace and grit, one small yes at a time, and I've changed my own little corner of the world in the process.

And you can too. What are your dreams, hopes and desires? Whether expressed or not, you have them. They may be sitting in the corners of your childhood memories or crying for attention at the center of your grown-up thoughts. This is the start of following your calling. Whatever your calling might be, it deserves at least one small yes from you. Will you raise your hand and say yes to what you have been uniquely created to do in this world? We can do it together, one small yes at a time.

Yes to discovering your big calling.

Yes to facing the challenges that will come against your new plans.

Yes to the daily choices that will move you toward your calling.

Yes to the tools that will help you embrace your calling.

Yes to the unconventional decisions that will keep you focused on your calling.

Yes to the smallest courage to keep going in the darkest times.

Yes to saying "no more" when you need to rest.

In the coming pages, you will discover *your* own unique calling and learn how to navigate the early challenges that you can expect to face as soon as you make a decision to embrace your calling. I will share a real strategy for committing to the "Everyday Yes" and practical tips for prioritizing never-ending activities in the face of your real need for rest. I will show you that it's OK to be unconventional in what you say yes to and how sometimes the most artful yes is actually a no.

Remember my fascination with documentaries? My hope is that someday when I am scrolling Netflix, I will watch one about you. This 60-minute special will tell us how you said a brave yes to your calling and then yes to staying in the daily game of family and business life as you pursued it. We will learn how you said yes to the best things of life in the face of ongoing challenges and demands for your time. You'll tell us about your unconventional wisdom and how you learned what to say yes to and about those occasions when you wisely said no. But most importantly, we will hear about the small moments where you said yes *just one more time* in the eleventh hour–when you had all but given up hope on yourself and your calling–and then you made it one more mile, one more day, one more time.

At the end of your show, they will ask you, "So tell us: How did you do it?"

And you will reply with a smile that I'm confident is meant just for me and say, "I did it one small yes at a time."

*Chapter 1*

# Finding Your "Yes"

*Y*es. Three little letters with big impact. The word yes is an initiator, an activator and a commitment to something tangible. A yes can be a promise of the heart or a proclamation to the world. Whether it's an internal or external affirmation, saying yes to something leaves a mark on you, the people you touch and the world you live in.

So the question is: "What kind of mark will you leave?"

Everyone is called to leave a mark on this world, but not all people will do it. The excuses are plentiful: I don't have the knowledge, time, resources, connections, education or influence. My kids are too little, my job is too big, my cash is too low, my debt is too high. I don't even know what I would do. I'm not big enough, smart enough, strong enough, brave enough, organized enough or disciplined enough.

1

Enough!

YOU. ARE. ENOUGH.

You have been equipped with everything you need to do what you have been created to do. Not all at once, of course. Not in one day or even one year. But one baby step, one small yes decision at a time, you can make steady progress towards making a mark in the world that is uniquely yours to make.

If you want to make a difference in your life or business, understanding your calling is key. Without it, you cannot make the mark on the world that you, and you alone, were intended to make. So what is the thing that keeps you up at night, that chases you while you sleep and that plays at the edges of your waking thoughts, quietly nudging you for more attention? What would you pursue if you had no constraints on your time and plenty of resources for the journey ahead?

You may refer to this mark you want to make on the world as a/an:

Dream

Idea

Goal

Vision

Hope

Target

Mission

Objective

Project

Duty

Ambition

But I refer to it as YOUR CALLING. Dreams, ideas and goals can change over time. Hope can be dashed and projects can be shelved. Vision can cloud and targets can move. Ambition can be lost. Missions can be rewritten and duties can shift. But a CALLING? That is different. A calling cannot be denied. A calling will keep after you until you answer it.

## Discovering Your Calling

Your calling has been hard-wired into your DNA. If you don't believe me, all you have to do is look to your childhood to realize that a calling has left a trail of clues from your earliest memories to the present day. What did you play as a young child? How did you spend your free time? What subjects did you enjoy in school? What shows did you watch? What made you angry? What made you smile? What got you into trouble? Just like the fairytale *Hansel and Gretel* your calling has left a path of clues. You just have to follow the path home.

I remember when my calling became clear to me. But it didn't start out that way. I was a 20-year-old college student, working my way through a Spanish degree by teaching dance lessons at a variety of local studios and a Boys & Girls Club. Although I enjoyed learning Spanish, I had no plans to teach it, and I wasn't sure what else one would do with a Spanish degree. I had managed a 4.0, but had not managed to make any meaningful relationships as a commuter student at my college. I was looking for a way out.

Out of desperation, I did the most logical thing my brain could think of at the time and made a list of all the possible things I thought I could do with my life. The only thing that interested me was the first item on the list: "Become a professional dancer."

I envisioned myself at the barre for daily classes and sweating through hours of company rehearsals. I could almost smell the theater and see the bright lights on the stage. To be honest, I don't know if I was convinced I actually wanted to be a dancer or if I was just convinced I didn't want to be a college student any longer. Either way, I set my eyes on the bright lights of New York City.

Before I go any further, I need to set the stage a bit. For starters, this was the mid-90s. I had no internet and no cell phone. I was still waiting for hours in line at the university computer lab to type papers for school, papers that were produced on a dot-matrix printer. I had no technology to my benefit and no resume to my credit, but I did have a worn-out copy of *Dance* magazine listing audition dates for a training program at the Alvin Ailey American Dance Center in NYC. Somehow, without a cell phone or internet, I found a flight and just enough courage to walk into one of the most famous dance schools in America and audition for their nine-month training program.

After an intense audition—one where they lost my paperwork and I was the last one waiting in the lobby for results—I got the answer I had hoped for: acceptance!

I envisioned my admission to the nine-month program as the first step towards my only goal of becoming a professional dancer. So when I heard weeks later that the Ailey Company was performing two hours away from my hometown, I made the drive to catch a sneak peek of what I was sure would be my future.

I was sitting solo in the theater watching the athleticism and artistry come to life in Ailey's most iconic piece, "Revelations", when suddenly my life's true purpose came into focus as I heard a gentle whisper in my heart, a quiet question asking me, "This is great, but how much of this performance will you remember a year from now, compared with how your students will remember the classes you gave and what you will remember of what you gave them?"

I slid down in my seat as tears filled my eyes. The truth was clear. I wouldn't remember the details of that performance in the years to come, but the students I had been teaching every day would remember my daily encouragement for a lifetime. I realized I had been chasing a dream to dance and ignoring my calling to teach.

As the final curtain fell, I rose from my seat. I knew what I needed to do. I don't remember much of that drive home, but I do remember using the phone in our kitchen to dial the Ailey school the next day to tell them I wouldn't be coming.

My calling was clear. The classroom would be my stage.

I have followed that calling for almost 20 years, one small yes at a time, and it has become more than I ever could have hoped for or imagined. Over the course of almost two decades, I've seen lasting benefits from encouraging my students in the classroom and beyond, mentoring them to use their gifts and talents to serve the community. My family has enjoyed the flexibility that comes with being self-employed, and they have learned from the sacrifices an entrepreneur must make. My employees have gained meaningful work along with full benefits–a situation that has given them the ability to focus on *their* calling for teaching. My business has raised more than $400,000 for the local Red Cross and provided more than $250,000 in scholarships to students and teachers and donations to various local causes. I have contributed funds to a new community theater and have partnered with the Boys & Girls Club where I first started teaching. My dance studio affiliation program has helped hundreds of studio owners save their businesses and become deeply involved in their own communities. Last month, more than 1 million students interacted with our online magazine that promotes positive messages to young dancers.

I have to admit that if I hadn't said that one small yes to my calling in the back of the theater all those years ago, tens of thousands of kids would not have been told "You have great worth and value as a human being" in our classrooms. Hundreds of thousands of dollars in scholarships and community grants would not have been funded through my business, and hundreds of dance studio owners would still be struggling to run successful businesses. And millions of dancers around the globe would be missing out on helpful and encouraging messages online, the place where most spend the majority of their free time. If I hadn't said that one small yes to pursue my calling to teach dance all those years ago, which then led to opening my own dance studio, my family, my employees, my community and the industry I work in would look a lot different.

Having a strong sense of calling is critical in creating a life of significance. If you know what you love to do or what you feel you were created to do, you will have the ability to make a bigger impact on the world because you will be working from a position of confidence rather than hopes and dreams. You will be building your life from a place of strong identity in who you are, instead of wearing other people's expectations or interests like a pair of bad-fitting jeans. You have a calling that fits *you*, and only you, and it is the key to making a difference that only you can make.

## Identity Crisis

When I was chasing the dream of becoming a professional dancer instead of my calling to become a teacher, I was experiencing an identity crisis. Perhaps you have faced a similar situation and you have put your stock into something you DO instead of someone you ARE. Your calling, that thing that only you can do in this world, is connected to who you ARE, not necessarily what you DO.

This might seem like an obvious difference, but think for a moment how foreign this distinction is in our daily language. Imagine this scene with me: You are at a reception and you are meeting someone for the first time. After the usual exchange of names and pleasantries, the very next question is going to be, "So what do you do?"

The mind has an innate desire to sort information. We are wired to put things, and people for that matter, into categories: safe/unsafe; interesting/boring; friend/foe. It's a modern version of self-preservation. We may no longer be running from bears or other predators in the wild, but there is still a food chain and our natural instinct is to find out where we fall on the hierarchy as fast as possible.

All of this information sorting, however, has led us to an identity crisis of sorts. We not only categorize other people by what they do, we identify ourselves by our activities as well. Let's unpack this a little deeper for a minute.

Here's a list of what I DO on a regular basis:

1. I run a dance studio for 750 kids.
2. I coach 164 dance studio owners around the globe.
3. I write articles for magazines.
4. I give keynote speeches.
5. I attend board meetings.
6. I chauffeur my kids around.
7. I eat dinner with my family.
8. I go to church on Sundays.

That's what I DO most of the time, but here's who I AM all of the time:

1. I am a teacher.
2. I am a business coach.
3. I am a writer.
4. I am a communicator.
5. I am a volunteer.
6. I am a parent.
7. I am a wife.
8. I am a child of God.

If my dance school goes away, I would teach something else because I am still a teacher by nature. If I decided to stop coaching studio owners,

I would coach other business owners. I'm no longer writing only for magazines, and if I never give another keynote I would still be wired as a communicator. I don't need a stage to make a speech; just ask my kids. I can't really wrap my head around it at this point in my life, but someday my kids will go off to college. I'll still always be a parent and a wife. But, most importantly to me, even if I never had the chance to go to church again, I would always be one of God's kids.

Take a minute and read the following sentence out loud: Who you ARE is as important to your CALLING as your calling is to creating a life that makes a DIFFERENCE in the world. Now, let it really soak in. Do you see the math inside of that sentence? Here is the formula for you visual learners like me:

Who you are = your calling

Your calling = the difference you were made to make in this world

Sometimes it's easier to see this equation in the lives of other people than it is to see in our own lives. Take Walt Disney for example. Walt Disney was created to, well, create! He said yes to his calling and raised enough money on his own to build the "Happiest Place on Earth," despite a lack of support from his board of directors and even his own brother. WHAT he did was build Disney World; WHO he was, however, was a creative genius. Had he not said yes to his calling, 650 million people would not have experienced the wonder of imagination and discovery within its gates, and central Florida would likely still be swampland. Even if you have never visited one of Disney's theme parks, his characters were probably some of the most recognizable figures of your childhood.

Let's take a look at another recognizable world figure, Mother Teresa, a woman wired with a servant heart. She said yes to her calling to help the poorest of the poor, unwanted and unloved throughout society. WHAT she did was found a new religious community; WHO she was at heart was a messenger of charity. Had she not said yes to her calling, countless people would have suffered lonely, undignified lives and deaths. In 2011, I visited her Home for the Destitute and Dying in Haiti. I encountered profound peace there, despite being in the midst of some of the most heartbreaking situations I had ever witnessed. Had Mother Teresa not said yes in India over a half-century earlier, these men and women in Haiti would have been spending their last days in the garbage-covered streets outside.

Another significant leader, Abraham Lincoln, was a man innately tuned into issues of equality and justice. He said yes to acting on a deep conviction against what he called the "monstrous injustice of slavery." WHAT he did was abolish slavery using his position as president of the United States; WHO he was at his core was a brilliant mediator. If he had not said yes to his calling and written the Emancipation Proclamation—even without the support of his most trusted advisors—who knows how long it would have taken to get the 13th Amendment, ending slavery in the U.S.

And then there was Alex Scott, a young girl diagnosed with a neuroblastoma—a type of childhood cancer—who decided at age four to start a lemonade stand to help other kids fight cancer. WHAT she did was raise more than $1 million dollars to help find a cure for the disease that ultimately took her life at the age of eight. WHO she was, however, was an advocate for others. Had she not said yes to her calling, the additional $121 million dollars raised to date by Alex's Lemonade Stand Foundation for Childhood Cancer would not be funding pediatric cancer research today.

Don't let the famous stories fool you. It's not the size of the outcome that determines the value of your calling. Not all callings play out in the same way. My friend Carmen left her job as a hairdresser to homeschool her children, an arrangement that gives her more time to volunteer in the housing projects not far from her home. Carmen is called to be a caretaker. Her best friend, Angela, gave up her time at home to take on a full-time job in order to help provide for her family. Angela is also called to be a caretaker, but the way she answers her calling–or "what she says yes to"–looks different than Carmen's does. And that is just how it should be. Had each of them not said yes to their callings in the way that they did, their children would not be the confident, capable young people they are today. Your calling, and how you say yes to it, is yours and yours alone.

## Your Calling Leaves Clues

Earlier I told you that a calling has been hard-wired into your DNA. Reflecting on your life thus far, you can find clues to your calling. What you played with, watched, did and made in your free time as a child are clues. How you have spent your time and money are more clues. So are the things that made you happy and got you fired up. Or, more interestingly, what was that thing you got into trouble because you just couldn't help but do it? That can be a clue to your calling as well.

I want to introduce you to my best friend, Alana, who also happens to be my younger sister by ten years. As a child, every parent-teacher conference was a dreaded event for Alana. It didn't matter the teacher, subject or grade level, the conversation always went something like this:

"She talks too much in class."

"She's too social."

"She doesn't follow the rules."

"She can't sit still."

For most of her life, Alana was told she was a little too chatty, a little too loud and had a little too much difficulty doing things the school's way. All of it was a nice way of saying she didn't follow the rules. Alana marched to the beat of her own drum and school wasn't on her playlist, so she opted out of college and went straight into sales.

Twenty years ago, those teacher observations were presented as problems. Today, we understand them as clues to her calling. Alana now enjoys a thriving career in national sales and is the author of a successful blog called, Tiny Traveler–a chronicle of her adventures travelling 50,000 miles a year for a sales career with a baby in tow.

Guess what, folks? WHAT Alana does is TALK for a living, and it reflects WHO she is: a social, independent thinker. Had she not leaned into her natural gifts and pursued a career in sales, she would probably still be bumping up against people who would be telling her to pipe down, and she wouldn't be living the rich, fulfilling life she is today. Alana's story is an example of what can happen when you find your calling and say yes to who you really are.

## Beginner Blues

As a teen and young adult, I had this recurring thought: "I'm good at a lot of things, but I'm not GREAT at anything." When I decided to answer my calling to open a dance studio, those thoughts resurfaced, throwing fear of inadequacy over all of my ambitious plans. Sure, I was a capable dancer, but I knew I wasn't the best in my class. I had a good head for numbers, but no accounting background. I knew how to write term papers, but not contracts. And for pity's sake, I had a Spanish degree, not a business degree, or even a dance degree. I felt totally ill-equipped for the race ahead before I ever got to the starting blocks–a real recipe for the "beginner blues."

Then I realized that I wasn't alone. Remember my obsession with the biographies of interesting and successful people? I had already been inspired by learning about what they had accomplished one small yes at a time. There was another common–and perhaps even more encouraging–denominator that I found among the achievers I admired: Most of them didn't know what they were doing when they started either! Remembering this gave me hope back then, and it still gives me hope every time I suffer from a case of the beginner blues.

Consider the following people whose humble beginnings didn't match their eventual end games. Media magnate Martha Stewart was a stockbroker turned homemaker/caterer before she became an authority on elegant living. Mark Cuban of Shark Tank did stints as a bartender and salesperson before building the software company that made him a billionaire. JK Rowling's writing experience prior to publishing the Harry Potter series was as a secretary–and a clinically depressed, unemployed one at that. I've never had a personal conversation with any of these people, but I've read enough about them to know they didn't wake up one day fully equipped to pursue their calling. Even Moses, though clearly called to action by a burning bush, had only one response to God: "I'm not qualified." Still, each of these people summoned the courage to tackle their fears, objections and rejections one small yes at a time–just like you and I must do.

Humble beginnings, false starts and setbacks can make you doubt yourself or make you think you are going in one direction when you should be going another. The beginning blues are not to be avoided. They are necessary to reaffirm your calling. Remember, dreams and ideas can change over time. Hope can be dashed and projects can be shelved. Missions can be re-written and duties can be shifted, but a calling cannot be denied. If you are truly called to do something, you will continue to say yes even when you don't feel up to the task.

## Personality Positions

I belong to a CEO group that meets twice a year for trainings. One of the most interesting things I've observed in the four years we've been meeting, is how personality has an impact on the way people say yes to their callings. Marc, one of my colleagues in the group, has the nickname "Spark Speed." True to his personality, if he feels led to do something, it will be done tomorrow and it will be packaged in spectacular fashion. His philosophy is that if you are going to make mistakes you might as well get out there and make them big and fast. Brad, another member of the group, takes a more pragmatic approach. The phrase you will hear him say most often about trying new concepts is "bullets before cannonballs."

Depending on our personalities, saying yes to our calling and creating a life that makes a difference can either go one way or another. For example, when Marc built his first software company, he didn't even own a computer, but as a venture capitalist he recognized the product was a winner, so he said yes to figure the rest out. When Brad started his toy manufacturing company, he already had a wealth of ideas from years spent working in his industry, so he said yes to building on his knowledge base and experience. For each personality it's different, but what's universal is that if either of them hadn't followed their calling, they would not be making the impact on their employees and communities that they are today. Marc's personality just requires him to do it one way, and Brad's personality requires him to do it a different way.

Your personality has just as much impact on how you approach saying yes to what *you* have been called to do as it does for my colleagues and me. Your personality also affects how fast–and how smooth–you are going to get to where you want to go. Consider the following small snapshots of personality types:

Quick start vs. jump-start

Sprint racer vs. marathon runner

Possibility seeker vs. problem finder

Detail planner vs. spontaneous decision maker

Penny pincher vs. big spender

Flexible vs. rigid

Internal processor vs. external processor

Kite vs. string

This is by no means an exhaustive list, but if you were planning a trip, this short personality profile would reveal a lot about how you like to travel. That's why it's important to understand that the personality traits you will carry with you on your one small yes journey can be your best ally...or your worst enemy. The big idea here is to match your personality, as much as you can, to how you say yes.

Let me pause here and say that I don't believe that any of the above personality traits are inherently better or worse, right or wrong. God has clearly made several different types of people and I believe He knew exactly what He was doing when He created YOU. But if you know you lean towards a particular way of thinking or handling opportunities and obstacles, it's smart to know that ahead of time so you can build in some strategies to protect yourself from the downsides of each personality type.

If you lean towards needing a jump-start and require frequent rest breaks, adjust your pace and path now before you start. Perhaps you are the detail-oriented person who falls apart when things don't go as planned. If that's you, what you need to plan for most is getting comfortable with the inevitable changes ahead. If you are a spontaneous sprinter, you might move faster than the rest of us, but you are also likely to be off track as much as you are on. If that's you, remember that not all activity is progress.

When you understand the role personality can play on how you say yes to your calling, you will be better prepared to go the distance as you create a meaningful, joyful life.

## One Small Yes

Everyone is called to make some kind of unique mark in this world, but not all people will do it. You, my friend, are not all people. For starters, you bought this book and you made it through the end of the first chapter. Do you know how many people buy books and never even get that far? The Japanese even have a word for it: Tsundoku, which means "buying books and letting them pile up unread." That's not you! You are not only going to read this book, you are going to mark it up like crazy with notes and insights.

There may be days when you will still confuse who you are with what you do. There will be times when you will feel ill-equipped for what you have been called to do. You might even be tempted to give up before you start. But you won't quit because you will be prepared.

Your personality may make you want to hand over the job of pursuing your calling to someone else, but no one can pursue your calling for you. I can't do it. Your parents can't do it. Neither can your neighbor, best friend, kids or spouse. It's yours. You have to do it. Are you ready to start?

All it takes is one small yes from you.

Yes?

Let's go!

## Chapter 2

# The Challenge of Yes

The easiest part is done. You have made the first of many small yes declarations you will make to yourself on this journey. Now comes the Challenge of Yes, which in my experience goes something like this: I've finally put down my excuses and said yes to what I feel I've been called to accomplish in this world. I revel in the certainty of my decision for a short time and then...bam! Challenges, distractions and even my own habits start throwing roadblocks in the way of following through on my new commitment.

Sound familiar? This chapter is about the challenges that come along with saying yes to your calling. Embracing your calling will be hard, no doubt, but you must say yes to the challenges if you want to build a business and a life that make a difference. In this chapter we'll go through the challenges you can expect to face after you embrace your calling and how they can actually affirm your calling.

Challenges to your resolve can come in many different shapes and forms. Let's begin with some common challenges to expect once you've said your first small yes to your calling. By the end of this chapter you will know what to expect and how to say yes to tackle these challenges head on. You will also be able to face them with a greater sense of calm and resolve when they DO come (and they will) because you will be prepared.

## Challenge #1: Opportun-itis

"Opportun-itis" might not be a real word, but it is a very real condition–especially for those who naturally tend toward an "anything is possible" mindset. In fact, the very same personality trait that makes a person quick to say yes to their calling can also make it easy to say yes to opportunities that might NOT be in line with their calling.

Have you ever said yes to something only to have another exciting opportunity come along right on the heels of your recent commitment? I have and it almost always gives me a case of opportun-itis–a wacky feeling that the new opportunity might somehow be better than what I just said yes to and that if I don't pursue this "new thing" right now I will never have the chance again. Never! (Opportun-itis is a cousin to drama.)

Opportun-itis may be irrational, but it's not infrequent. I've experienced it many times. Most recently, we were struggling to keep our new online magazine for students afloat. We had been plugging away faithfully for about nine months with only moderate results. Even though a good part of me wanted to fold the project for lack of traction, I still believed in the concept. It was decision time, so I made a commitment to my team to dig in and keep it going for another year.

A few months after I made that commitment in front of my team, I received a job offer from an incredible company. It was the second company to offer me an out-of-state executive position in less than a year. Opportun-itis kicked in. I wrestled mentally and emotionally with the proposal. The job would have been an easy way out of the situation I had gotten myself into with the barely-above-failing online magazine and a big step up both financially and opportunity-wise. But in the end I turned it down. I chose to honor my first yes, not just to the online magazine, but to all of my businesses, and to the employees and clients who depended on our services.

The funny thing is that almost immediately after I chose not to pursue the most recent opportunity, one article went viral and the fledgling website took off. We went from getting a few thousand site visits to more than 200,000 site visits in one month. Our social media interactions went from about 10,000 to more than 1 million in that same time period. If I had given up on my calling to say yes to something that wasn't my calling at the time, I would have been quitting right before the breakthrough.

The important thing to remember is that if you pursue every opportunity that comes your way, you will never follow through on the ONE that is just right for you. I've come up with a saying to help keep myself on track when opportun-itis strikes:

"Not all GOOD things are GREAT things;
not all GREAT things are GOD things;
not all GOD things are RIGHT NOW things."

Just because something is a GOOD idea in general, doesn't mean it's a GREAT idea for you. Even if the idea is GREAT, it might not be that very best thing that GOD has planned for your life. Even if it is what I would call a God-thing–something you believe you were absolutely made to do or be a part of–it might not be a RIGHT NOW thing. Keeping opportun-itis in check is essential if you are going to embrace your calling.

## Challenge #2: Doubter's Default

If opportun-itis is the affliction of the hopeful, doubt is the affliction of the fearful. Have you ever had any of these thoughts? "I believe I am called to do this amazing thing, but I'm not sure I can actually do it." Once the "I'm not sure I can do it" door is opened, it can quickly swing wide to "I'm pretty sure I can't do it at all." If that happens you are in the "doubter's default" position.

For most of Crystal's career she feared failure. As a young studio owner, she operated squarely from the doubter's default position, filling her head with thoughts like:

"You CAN'T start an honor society chapter for your students."

"You CAN'T add that program because no one will register."

"You could NEVER host your recital at an expensive theatre because you can't afford it."

"You will NEVER have a big school because your market is saturated."

After attending a member rally for our affiliated studios, Crystal made the conscious decision to start replacing fear with knowledge and confidence. For three years she faced her doubts one small yes at a time. This year all of her small yeses added up to a great result as she inducted an entire class of students into her own chapter of the National Honor Society for Dance Arts–something she had previously considered out of her reach.

Crystal still faces the normal fears that come with being self-employed and a mom, but she doesn't let them rule her any more. She has built her confidence with each small yes over the past three years and today she is leading a large dance studio that makes a difference in her community. To hear Crystal speak now is like listening to a different person than the one I met three short years ago. I have actually heard her say, "Yes, you can start a whole program from scratch! Yes, you can get the congresswoman from your state to be a speaker at your honor society induction. YES you can! I've said yes to new promotions, yes to trying new ways to generate revenue, yes to correcting staff when I hate confrontation and yes to working on our studio culture. My studio is so much better because of each small YES."

Crystal isn't alone in her one small yes journey. All of us will face fear and doubt as we step out to pursue things that matter to us. Most of the significant and worthwhile things I've done in my life would be classified as scary on some level. Getting married, having children, becoming self-employed, walking away from a performing career and other professional opportunities have all created moments of insecurity. The idea here is not to eliminate all fear and doubt. The emotions of fear and doubt have a place in the one small yes journey because they are regulators causing us to think twice before agreeing to do something. The key is to keep fear and doubt in their proper place as caution lights, not as red lights that will keep us from moving forward with our calling.

## Challenge #3: Distraction-Actions

If you haven't encountered this challenge yet, you will soon because everyone has a "distraction-action" they will go to when they don't want to do the real work that comes with saying yes to their calling. It's in our human nature to want to do the easiest thing first. Listen closely when I say that this is one of the biggest challenges I have to fight every day on my say-yes journey.

For example, if there are ten things on my to-do list—eight easy, low-value tasks and two difficult, but high-value tasks—I naturally want to do the eight easy, low-value projects first because I like the sense of accomplishment that comes with checking a lot of things off my list. In fact, I like checking things off so much that I've even added items to my list that were already done just for the satisfaction of crossing them off. Now that's when you know you have a problem with distraction-actions.

Small, low-value task items are seductive because it's in our nature to want to finish things and we feel unsettled when we don't. Psychologists call this the Zeigarnik Effect or the tendency to want to complete what is incomplete. This is such a strong part of our psychology that we will unconsciously choose to pursue tasks we are confident we can complete in a given time frame, even if they are not in alignment with our big picture goals.

Let's go back to the list of ten tasks. Imagine that you've somehow managed to check off the eight small, low-value tasks. All you have left on your list now are two really important and meaningful projects that if accomplished will change the course of your business, career, family or relationships. With only two things left on your list, and both of them high impact, what do you think the next most likely thing is that you will do? Will you tackle the two life-altering projects?

Probably NOT.

If you have already spent your day checking off small, low-value tasks, you are much more likely to start some new low-value task–like tidying up your desk, cleaning the kitchen or making a post for your business Facebook page–instead of tackling the remaining two difficult, but high-value tasks.

Here is the hard truth: In the absence of easy-to-complete options, we often create our own distraction-actions in order to avoid starting a task that is perceived as difficult or one we don't think can be finished in one sitting. Even if we are close to the finish line, having accomplished eight of the ten things on our list, we will then go fuss with some other unnecessary small task rather than start on a bigger, more meaningful task. Why do we do this? Because we are wired to believe there is no use starting a big project at 2 p.m. because it can't be finished before we leave for the day. The end result is that we often go to bed having done a lot but not having accomplished anything of substance.

UCLA's beloved basketball coach John Wooden was often quoted as saying to his players, "Do not mistake activity with achievement." Whether you are a basketball player, a student, a stay-at-home mom or an entrepreneur, it's important to remember that not all activity is created equal. Spending time on your distraction-actions is just an exhausting version of procrastination that will keep you from ever getting the real job done. If you want to create a life or a business that makes a difference, you must continually say yes to the projects that are in line with your calling in the midst of challenges from distraction-actions and other low-value tasks.

## Challenge #4: Low-D

Merriam-Webster has six definitions for the word discipline, or "D," as I call it. I have only one: "Discipline is the routine I must have to save myself from myself." Left to my own devices, I really wouldn't get much done. In fact, a low-D day might look something like this for me:

| | |
|---|---|
| 8 a.m. - | Wake up. Go back to bed. |
| 9 a.m. - | Wake up for real. Check email on my phone from the warmth of my blankets. I live in Wisconsin so this is justified. |
| 9:30 a.m. - | Eat sausage and pancakes–possibly in bed. |
| 10 a.m. - | Do some "research" for my dance studio business on Facebook–long research with several detours to watch motivational videos about dancing cats in other countries. |
| 12 p.m. - | Go to Rudy's Drive-In where I will reward all of my research efforts with a bucket of batter-fried cheese curds and a root beer float. Maybe two. |

1 p.m. -  Continue exploring my business interests on YouTube followed by some dedicated time to Tiny House, Big Living on HGTV. After all, that tiny house I want to build isn't going to build itself now will it? These things take dedication!

4 p.m. -  Eat dinner out with my family because cooking would mess up the kitchen.

5 p.m. -  Put the children to bed early so that I can continue my contributions to the greater world on Instagram or possibly visit my dance studio if I'm not too tired from the day's work.

Just kidding—but not really. In the absence of the discipline of routine I would most likely do whatever lazy thing pleased me all day long. I've often been told, "Misty, you are so disciplined about everything you do. You must LOVE discipline." The truth is that I don't like discipline any more than my children do, but I REALLY like the results of discipline, so I keep fighting off low-D and creating routines that will make me, my family and my business strong.

My actual average day is much less exciting, and much less tasty, than the low-D day above. Prepare to be amazed by the boringness.

5:30 a.m. -  Wake up. Get up. Quiet time in my office, review of day ahead and respond to overnight messages.

6: 30 a.m. -  Kids up for school. Oatmeal or yogurt.

7: 30 a.m. -  Check social media traffic for all businesses and do a short workout for flexibility or strength.

8 a.m. -  In office working on number one priority.

11:30 a.m. -  Lunch. Usually leftovers because I don't like to cook.

12 p.m. -  More work on number one priority followed by emails and calls.

| | |
|---|---|
| 3 p.m. - | If I'm working at home, it's break time when the school bus shows up. If I'm working in the office, it's one final push on the number one priority. |
| 5 p.m. - | Dinner with kids, kids' activities, homework, bath time and bedtime. Screens off. |
| 8 p.m. - | Wrap up in office or visit the dance studio. |
| 10 p.m. - | Hang out with my husband, read or watch a Tiny House show. |
| 11 p.m. - | Sleep. |

Some days I work later or get up earlier. Some days I spend my day at the office and other times I work from home. One day I might go for a walk instead of doing yoga for exercise. I even tried jogging once for variety's sake. Once. If I'm really feeling crazy, I might even have a cup of buttered coffee to spice things up. Other than that it's a pretty predictable routine that saves me from my low-D tendencies.

Without D, I would still be dreaming about following my calling to open a dance studio, but saying yes to the discipline of routine has helped me to build a business and life that make a difference. I started the routine of discipline before I built my studio by saying yes to holding down three jobs while going to college to save enough money for the launch. Talk about a boring routine: work, school, homework, work, work. Repeat. My friends went out while I stayed home to work on a business plan. My friends bought clothes, but I bought leotards to sell in a studio that didn't exist yet. The routine was exhausting, but every day that I gave one small yes to another shift at one of the many jobs I had or one small yes to save money instead of spending my earnings took me closer to launch day.

You've probably noticed the routine I follow today isn't all that different from the routine I used to build my business almost 20 years ago. The routine itself is boring, but I want to be very clear that life is not. The routine doesn't enslave me; it saves me! I am free to enjoy my family and my business because the routine I have developed helps to contain the chaos that can accompany running a small business while raising a family. What I really value is being able to mentor students, give back to my community and spend time with my family. Having a routine helps me get the work of my calling done so I can spend time doing the other things I value.

If you are going to build a business and a life that will make a difference in the world, you will have to fight low-D as well. Anchor your day to routines that will minimize your chances of following the natural tendency to do-what-feels-good-now and maximize your ability to focus on things that will produce real results over time. How you spend your days determines what you make of your life. You only get to spend it once, so spend it well by saying yes to routine of discipline NOW so you can enjoy the results of your discipline LATER.

## Challenge #5: Blue-Sky Syndrome

One of my favorite things in the world is to have "blue-sky conversations" with other big-hearted entrepreneurs and out-of-the-box thinkers. I love talking about all that could be created to make the world a better place. It's the verbal equivalent of staring into a blue sky in the morning and dreaming of what the day could hold.

Emily is the biggest blue-sky thinker I have ever met. Since becoming her mentor three years ago, I have watched Emily follow her calling to move to a new town, buy a warehouse, build an amazing performing arts center, start a professional ballet education program and welcome a third child to her family–a sequence of events that would tire most people out just reading about it.

But in Emily's mind this is just the beginning of what she has been called to do. Since I've known her, she has added dream after dream to the list of things she would like to build and create as she follows her calling to change the lives of teens and her community.

Emily has no formal business training, but that doesn't deter her from pursuing the following blue-sky ideas:

- Opening five locations for her performing arts center.
- Building an amphitheater on her property.
- Starting a fair-trade dance shoe company.
- Creating an online leadership course for teens.
- Partnering with suppliers to build a virtual art supply store.
- Starting a folk music school for preschool students.

Emily also has her eyes on real estate, coaching and hosting a series of live events. Emily sees all of these ideas as a natural extension of the one small yes she said to her calling.

While Emily is the definition of all of the positive attributes of a blue-sky thinker, she would be the first to tell you that her ability to think big and move fast can be a two-edged sword. On one hand, she can see possibilities in such vivid detail that she is able to bring ideas to life with astounding speed. I've heard many people marvel at how much she gets done while having three small children at home.

On the other hand, Emily's interest in "what could be" has the constant potential to take her eyes off the value of "what already is." She knows that if she allows blue-sky thinking to rule her, blue-sky syndrome can kick in and cause her to run 100 miles an hour in ten different directions—getting nowhere while exhausting her resources, her family and her team.

Emily has learned to weigh each new opportunity against her calling in order to keep blue-sky syndrome in check so that her new ideas don't overwhelm the great things she already has going on in her life. This helps her to continually affirm her true calling so that she can be a person who makes a difference with her life and business, and not just a person who is very busy.

## Challenge #6: Intellectual Obesity

One of the most common things a person will do once they have said yes to a calling is research it ferociously. Part of that drive to research how to accomplish your calling is just good planning and preparation; it's smart to arm yourself with as much information as you can for the journey ahead. But another part of the motivation is simply to reassure yourself that what you've said yes to will be possible. A tiny part of the investigation might even be to look for a reason that pursuing your calling is NOT possible so you can go back to your regular life.

Researching how to follow your calling can take many forms. Between books and podcasts, Google and YouTube, conferences and online courses, you can learn, or become, virtually anything if you set your mind to it. As good as these things are, however, over-researching and over-planning can become a distraction from taking action. When you consume more information than you need, you run the risk of becoming "intellectually obese."

Have you ever heard the phrase "paralysis by analysis?" That's exactly what can happen if you get stuck too deep in the information cycle. With so many facts and figures, examples and opinions available at your fingertips, it's easy to go into information overload and shut down. Remember, information is only power if you use it.

In your quest to learn all you can about what you have decided to do, take care that you don't get caught in the trap of consuming too much information and using too little of it. Fighting this challenge will affirm your calling because you will be putting what you have learned into action. If you are going to continue saying yes to your calling it's more important to exercise what you already know than it is to know everything about where you are going.

## Challenge #7: Counting the Cost

When I met Julien, he had an established career at a university and was busy building a dance and fitness studio on the side. He spent his days teaching and recruiting adults on campus and his nights alongside his wife and their three small children at their studio. After three years of balancing the demands of two careers and a family, Julien felt it was time to make the leap and become completely self-employed.

He had attempted the move twice before but never felt the timing was right. The third time he was tempted to shy away because of fear of failure or putting his family at risk. "Who am I to limit God in what he can do?" he thought. If entrepreneurship was really his calling it was time to pursue it. Julien jumped.

At first things went really well for Julien. With his energy renewed, he focused 100 percent of his attention on growing the small business and making more time for family–something he had missed while working his university job and running the studio at the same time. He made steady strides as a business owner towards building a life he loved where he was in control of his time and financial future.

But soon Julien was having so much fun in entrepreneurship that he decided to build another business less than a year after taking on his first business full time. His new idea would combine his experiences in adult education at the university with his passion for entrepreneurship to teach adults how to find their own path in business and life, just as he had done.

Julien shifted his focus from his studio and put most of his time and energy into the new endeavor. In a very short period of time he authored a book and launched a podcast that hit the New & Noteworthy list on iTunes. After that success, he partnered with an online community builder to build a new site called Sleep Sumo. Julien was an entrepreneur on fire!

That's great for Julien, right?

Wrong.

Life quickly became harder for Julien and his family than it had been when he was balancing a day job and building his first business. At least when he was straddling the university and self-employment, he had the security of a paycheck to count on if his small business didn't go as planned. But being an author-podcaster-online community builder cost more time and money than he imagined, and this second foray into entrepreneurship put unbelievable pressure on his first small business.

Julien simply didn't "count the cost" of the new venture–a cost to his time, health, relationships and primary business. He eventually sold his house to cover the expenses he incurred while on entrepreneurial overdrive, put his podcast on hold, shut down the Sleep Sumo site and woke up to the beauty of what he had originally said yes to–a dance and fitness business and a family that he loved.

There is a cost to pursuing your yes, a cost to not pursuing it and a cost to getting off track. Julien's story is a great reminder to count the cost of your yes before you start. If you are going to say yes to the calling that is right for your life, you must count the physical, emotional, financial and relational cost of every yes.

## Challenge #8: Finding the Best Yes

When I was a teen it seemed like so many of the decisions I faced were "good vs. bad" decisions.

"Should I go out to a party or stay home and study on Friday night?"

"Should I own my mistake and get in trouble or tell a lie to avoid consequences?"

"Should I buy that thing on credit or should I save and buy it with money I've already earned?"

As I've grown older, I've faced fewer of the clearly good and bad decisions and more of the gray "good, better, best decisions." It's not the thought of sorting out what to do on Friday night that makes me think twice nowadays; it's Tuesday nights that challenge me to find the "best yes" decision. Take this recent Tuesday for example:

It was 5 p.m. I'd been working all day, but the work for my business was nowhere near done. I was also on deadline for an article for a magazine, and my son had soccer practice in 30 minutes.

I could only spend the next 60 minutes one way and there was no clear right or wrong answer as to which activity should get a yes from me. In a case like this, and so many others we face as adults, it's important to find the BEST yes.

Going back to the Tuesday 5 p.m. example, let's imagine that the work was not due for two more weeks, the article could be written after bedtime, and I hadn't seen a soccer practice yet this season. In that case, finishing work would have been OK, but heading out to the fields would be the best yes decision.

But let's say that the unfinished work was returning a call from an upset client, the article was due at midnight and there were six more weeks of soccer. In this situation, it would have been best to take a few minutes to calm the client, finish the article and then mark my calendar for the next week's soccer practice. Nobody wants to miss out on family time, but would I really have been "present" if I were emotionally chewing on the client issue and writing the article in my mind while watching drills?

In the past, I've tried to avoid making difficult decisions in order to keep everybody happy, but that made nobody happy in the process, including myself. If you are going to run hard after your calling, you will need to learn to find the best yes decisions amidst all the good and great things that vie for your time and attention each day.

You will experience many challenges as you embrace your calling. But they aren't there to deter you; they will affirm your calling and help you make the best decisions to create a life and business with meaning. I've identified eight challenges that are common to embracing your calling. You likely will face each of these, and many others, as you work to make the mark that you and only you can make on this world.

Don't avoid, dodge or short-circuit the strength-training opportunity that comes from saying yes to facing these challenges. The challenges will help you stay true to your calling. Embrace the challenges.

Choose to fight opportun-itis, doubter's default, low-D, blue-sky syndrome and intellectual obesity so that they don't keep you from following through on your new commitment to your calling. Count the cost of each decision you make, and work to find the best yes option in every situation. In doing so, you will develop the focus, confidence, discipline, routines and knowledge to make a life and business that make a difference.

Just tackle each challenge one small yes at a time.

## Chapter 3

# The Everyday Yes

*E*very small yes choice from morning to night has an impact on the progress you will make towards your calling. It's the small yes to get up a half an hour earlier than usual so that you can get your day organized before the kids wake up or a small yes to eating breakfast before rushing out the door so that you'll have energy to start the day. It's the small yes to take the stairs instead of the elevator before sitting down to a day's work and another small yes to turn off the screens and shut down the troubles of the day before you get home.

There are endless examples of small yes decisions you make on a minute-by-minute basis during the day–most of which you make without ever really thinking about it. Our lives to a great degree are on autopilot in the 21st century. We get up, we go to work, we eat our meals, we watch TV and we go to bed. The next day the cycle repeats itself. Some days there are variations but for the most part people live their lives in an ongoing cycle of unconscious daily decisions, the effect of which is often not seen until the end of their lives.

Most people are very familiar with the concept of how compound interest works in banking. When you borrow money, compound interest works against you; and when you save money, it works in your favor. But what you might not have been taught in school is that there is also a compound interest effect in decision-making. Every small decision you make either moves you slowly toward or away from your goals. Darren Hardy, *New York Times* bestselling author of *The Compound Effect* and former publisher and founding editor of *SUCCESS Magazine,* sums it up this way, "The secret of your success is found in your daily routine."

In this chapter I will show you the importance of saying yes to your calling on a daily basis and how the small yes decisions in everyday life will impact whether or not you create a business and life that make a difference.

## "Life Wouldn't Be so Hard if it Weren't so Daily"

Early in my teaching career I was struggling to keep all the proverbial balls in the air. I would arrive to the dance studio at 7 a.m. and bring my breakfast, lunch and dinner with me so that I wouldn't have to take any breaks. As our company's sole administrator, any time I lost during the day would certainly mean having to make up for it after classes at the end of the night, so that meant eating my meals at my desk. Full days in the office were followed by full nights in the classroom. Every afternoon at 4 p.m., I would trade my street clothes for dance clothes and spend another five to six hours doing what I really wanted to do– teach children.

After spending a couple of years in this routine, I was on the edge of burnout. Nothing particular had gone wrong, but I was worn out from working around the clock and trying to keep everything running smoothly on my own. I shared a bit of my struggle with a friend who captured exactly what I was feeling in one sentence: "Life wouldn't be so hard if it weren't so daily." Isn't that the truth!

In that moment my mindset shifted and I understood that the most important part of pursuing my calling was NOT learning the technical skills of the business or keeping up with my dance training to stay relevant in the classroom, although that was necessary. The most important thing was simply to be CONSISTENT in doing the things that would get me where I wanted to go, even if they were routine, hard or boring at the time. When I had this realization, I stopped seeing the everyday activities of running a business as a grind and started seeing them as a strength-training workout for the life and business of meaning I wanted to have.

I realized that the strength training I was undergoing as a business owner wasn't all that different from the training I had endured as a dancer. When I was training as a dancer, I knew that the more consistent I was in the classroom, the stronger I would be on the stage. I suspected the same thing would happen to my business if I simply kept showing up each day to work the plan I had established.

My daily success habits as a young business owner were simple. Arrive early, answer messages, mail newsletters, create schedules, manage accounts, prepare for classes, teach classes, make phone calls and clean the studio for the next day. None of the tasks on the list were hard in and of themselves. Being consistent was the key to turning daily choices into future results.

The long days and continuous effort from all those years eventually paid off in mighty ways. Over time I was able to hire additional teachers for the classroom and help for the administrative tasks that were not my strengths. I still worked as many hours as I had before, but I was able to focus on my areas of passion, which in turn accelerated almost everything about the business. In time I was able to transition from leading the classroom to leading my team and ultimately from training my team to training other studio owners around the globe. What might have looked like overnight success to the outside world was actually 15 years of small yes decisions in the making.

## Real Strategy Required

Every small yes decision throughout your day can take you one small step further towards your calling, so it's important to get a real strategy to keep yourself on track. In the previous chapter I talked about how I have built routines into my life to save myself from myself. Here's a no-frills recap:

Wake up
Breakfast
Fitness
Working number one priority
Lunch
More work on number one priority
Communications
Family time
Final push on number one priority
Sleep

Because of this routine, I know what I'm going to do most days, but knowing what I'm going to do is only part of the solution. Actually getting myself to follow the routine requires a real strategy. Remember, if left to my own devices I would probably eat sausage and pancakes in bed while researching my calling on social media to avoid the hard work of actually fulfilling it. I know this about myself, so I have put strategies in place to make sure I follow each small part of the routine. These simple strategies will add up to big results over time.

My simple strategies begin anew every day. For example, my goal is to be up by 5:30 a.m. every day. To make sure that happens, I place the alarm clock on my chair. If I can reach the snooze button from the warmth of my pillow, I'm going to push it. Fitness requires an accountability partner, which for me right now is an online yoga boot camp. Eating right during the week means a trip to the grocery store on Sunday.

I also have a strategy to stay focused on my number one priority: have only one task on my desk at a time. My strategy to cover lunch is to eat leftovers and my strategy to stay focused on my family in the evening is to leave my phone in the car. My sleep strategy is to load an application on my computer that turns the screen a deeper and deeper shade of rose in the evening until it's no longer readable by the time I should go to bed. Eventually I tire of trying to read the screen and I close the laptop computer for the night. These strategies aren't fancy or complicated, just simple triggers I use to increase my chances of following the daily routine I set for myself.

The same strategies that allow us to accomplish our everyday routines in our personal life can be applied in business, too. For example, there are a few things I know I need to do every week to keep my business in shape. These activities include marketing our programs to the community, communicating with our teachers and clients, setting aside time to create new programs, developing trainings and reviewing our finances. I've developed a strategy of assigning each activity a focus day on my calendar. It's easier to remember to take time to communicate with and mentor my employees because I have an entire day on my calendar called "Tribe Tuesday." Assigning the core activities of my business to different days of the week helps me make sure they get accomplished regardless of the number of emails and interruptions that beg for my attention that day.

You can find more ideas for developing a strategy to accomplish your daily routine by downloading a free copy of the One Small Yes Daily Routine worksheet at onesmallyes.com

It's important to understand the significance of the everyday yes, but it's even more important to know yourself. What is easy for one person to say yes to day after day will be difficult for another. Real strategy is required to stay committed to the small choices that will move you towards your calling one day at a time. Connecting strategies to routines increases your chances of sticking to the things you have decided are important.

## Eat the Live Frog First

Not all small yes choices will have the same degree of difficulty for each person. For example, my husband has no problem throwing on his running shoes and pounding five miles of asphalt after a long day of work, but I know that if I don't exercise before noon I can write off the chance of it happening for the rest of the day. There is something about tackling the difficult activity in the morning.

Mark Twain said it best when he said, "Eat a live frog first thing in the morning and nothing worse will happen to you for the rest of the day." The same thing goes for your everyday yes decisions. Some of the decisions you need to make to build a life and business that you love will be natural for you and become automatic over time. Others will be a straight up struggle against your nature. If you know something is going to be a struggle, eat the live frog first, as Mark Twain suggested, before you do anything else in your day.

If anyone I know had a reason to stay in bed and avoid eating any live frogs for the day it was Hal Elrod. This young man had survived a horrific car crash–and died–only to be revived and face an arduous recovery. Physically weak and bitter with depression, Hal spent his days after the accident following his thoughts as they meandered through the successful career he previously enjoyed and what he was certain was the bleak road ahead.

Hal continued in this state for months, completely broken and nearly penniless, until a friend challenged him to get up at 5 a.m. and start each day by doing a little bit of the hard work required to get back on his feet. Hal wasn't an early riser by any stretch of the imagination, not even in his prior days as a successful salesman. But he accepted his friend's challenge and chose to eat the live frog. Hal got up early one day and then another and another. He moved his broken body and focused his thoughts through yoga and meditation. He repeated positive affirmations to himself even when his reality did not match the words he was saying.

All of those small, difficult, early-morning sessions added up to progress over time. The daily progress turned to passion, which eventually lead Hal to chronicle his experience in the number one best-selling book *The Miracle Morning: The Not-So-Obvious Secret Guaranteed to Transform Your Life (Before 8AM)*.

Hal has a calling to "transform millions of lives one morning at a time," and he is well on his way to doing it. With seven books, a podcast and a successful live event to his credit, Hal accomplishes his calling by doing the hard things first, one small yes and one morning at a time. If Hal had not eaten the live frog first all those mornings ago, hundreds of thousands of people would not be starting their days charged up to say yes to their own callings by 5 a.m.

## Mentors and Motivators

A person like Hal has the capacity to mentor hundreds of people in his lifetime and motivate millions. With the right relationships, style and frequency, mentors and motivators can help you continue to make one small yes strides toward your calling today and every day.

A mentor, by nature, is a person. It could be a person with whom you have a deep and personal relationship or a person whose wise counsel you have gleaned from reading her books and watching her example. Whether you acquire a mentor through personal relationship or professional admiration, you will benefit greatly from having a coach on your journey.

I have a few mentors without whom I would not be living the life I am today. If I have a big question or need direction on an important decision, one of the first things I will do is reach out to my mentors. If I have a question about how to navigate something in my current business I reach out to Dave. If the problem is with parenting, Karen is going to get the call. New entrepreneurial ideas get vetted though Paul, and I take my cues for a healthy marriage from Brad and Kelly. If I'm worried about a student, I'm going to ask Liz for perspective and insight. If my faith needs a charge, Michelle is the one I want to spend time with. Despite their busy lives, each of these people is always willing to share their wisdom from the trenches of business and life. Learning from their personal stories and insights has shaped my own life story. A good mentor can shape *your* story as well.

A motivator is different from a mentor. A motivator can be a person, but it could also be a video, a story, a podcast, a book, a movie, a webinar, a coaching program or an article in a magazine. While mentoring relationships are few and deep by nature, the spectrum of motivators is wide. A motivator requires no personal relationship, just access to information. If you like to learn by listening, subscribe to a motivational podcast. If you are more tactile, a webinar or book might be just the motivator for you. Do you need accountability? Find a coaching program with a proven track record of results to keep you moving toward your big picture calling.

Whatever your mentorship and motivation style, take the dose that is appropriate for you. I prefer to interact with mentors in person over shared meals or by working on projects together. Other people prefer to interact with their mentors in a classroom or a more formal meeting arrangement.

I digest motivation best in small daily doses anchored to my morning and evening routines. Other people prefer to binge motivate at week-long conferences and seminars. There is no right or wrong way, only a right way for you. The important thing is to build mentorship and motivation into your regular routines so that you can stay inspired and well-advised as you follow your calling.

## Permission Granted to Brake and Accelerate

Your calling is a DESTINATION and the act of saying yes to your calling every day is the VEHICLE to get you there. Just like with a vehicle, it's important to know when to put on the brakes and when to accelerate your yes.

My friend Brad once told me that good marriages are made up of two kinds of people—one is the gas pedal and the other is the brake. He went on to say that it's a beautiful arrangement as long as you don't push that brake and the gas pedal at the same time. Applying the gas and the brake at the right time makes for an exciting ride, but apply them at the same time and it is going to get rough pretty fast. There is a place for each one in life and relationships—just not at the same time.

Pursuing your calling is no different—if you want to have a smooth ride, you have to know when to put on the brakes and when to accelerate your yes. This is a lesson I have learned the hard way.

In my third year of business ownership I decided to open a second location for my dance studio. I ran the idea past my husband who not surprisingly vetoed it as a bad idea. His reasons were sound; I was pregnant with our second child, the business was still very young and we did not have the resources to keep a second location going if it were not successful within a very short period of time.

But I had no patience for his attempt to put the brakes on my brilliant idea. I decided that my reasons for saying yes were more compelling than his reasons for saying no. From my perspective, I had already proven I could establish and run a successful dance studio in one location, why couldn't I do it in another location just as well? I told myself that if I had been called to teach children, serving more children in more communities would certainly be better. I knew I didn't have the resources to keep it going if I didn't do most of the work myself, but I figured it was only five minutes down the road and it wouldn't be that hard to spread myself across the two locations.

I was wrong. Really wrong.

The location was a losing proposition from day one, and every layer of the project was a hassle. Teachers didn't want to drive to the second location and parents didn't want to sign up for classes there because I had more options at the first location. Expenses were high and enrollment was low. Not one to give in easily, I figured that the project just needed a little more acceleration from me. But the more yes I threw on the project–yes to more staffing, yes to more advertising, yes to more site visits–the more it became wrong for my family.

Still I kept my pedal to the metal through two years of frustration. In the end, I waved the white flag, admitted to my husband that he had been right all along, closed the doors and bought out the remainder of my lease. There was no price I wouldn't pay to regain control of my life at that point.

I'm not saying that opening a second location was a wrong idea in and of itself. But it was the wrong location, the wrong timing and it was wrong for my family. I spent two years accelerating when I should have been braking and another two years after that recouping the losses. I would consider opening a second location again, but it would have to be the right location, the right time and, most importantly, the right move for my family.

Looking back I realize I kept running ahead with my calling because I was afraid that if I didn't open a second location right then I would somehow fall behind in the marketplace. I didn't want to slow down my yes just because I was having a second child or lacked the resources. Instead of taking the few months I needed to recover from my second pregnancy and delivery, I spent four years recovering from a bad business decision.

In your commitment to making small yes choices to pursue your calling, you must balance your enthusiasm for progress with a real need to put the brakes on from time to time. You may even need to pivot instead of pushing on if you find yourself, like me, going in the wrong direction.

## 35,000 Decisions

Various internet sources estimate that an average adult makes 35,000 decisions each day. That's 35,000 opportunities to say yes to your calling. Imagine you had a bank account and every day you had 35,000 opportunities to put in a dollar. Wouldn't you focus 100 percent of your time and attention to making those deposits?

I would. And I think you would too.

But guess what? You have an even BETTER opportunity than the hypothetical one above. You have 35,000 chances a day to put MORE than a dollar in your bank account. You have 35,000 opportunities to take a one small yes step toward:

- Living a life that makes a difference.
- Building a business that you love.
- Making a mark on this world that is uniquely you.
- Laying a strong foundation to follow your calling.

And to think you were excited by the idea of giving 100 percent of your time and attention to making those dollar deposits. Money has a necessary place in your one small yes journey, but it pales in comparison to building a business and life that make a difference.

It is time to go all in. Every day. It's a challenge to show up every day and continually make small yes decisions to move your calling forward, so create a real strategy. It's not enough to know what you're going to do each day; you must be sure to actually do it.

Then get up each morning, look at the list of things you need to accomplish and eat the live frog first. Keep an eye on your speed during the day and take note of the road in front of you. There will be a time to push the gas and a time to hit the brake–but never at the same time.

This is the everyday yes–daily small yes choices that work like compound interest on your calling. Every day you have 35,000 opportunities to add little yes deposits to your calling, to become a little stronger, to work a little smarter and to get a little closer to the life you were meant to live. There is no better day to get started than today.

## Chapter 4

# The One Small Yes Toolbox

*"You have to have the right tool for the job."*
**– Paul Averill**

f I heard my dad say that phrase once while I was growing up, I heard him say it a thousand times. A truck driver by trade, my dad was a builder at heart. He spent years remodeling my childhood home before building a houseboat to cruise the Mississippi River with ease. When he was done with those projects he used his skills to build a playhouse for my sister. He also built kitchen cabinets, toy boxes, bookcases, gates and more. No matter the project, I always remember him saying, "Misty, you have to have the right tool for the job."

Your job, my friend, is to pursue your calling—that one thing that you and only you were created to do in this world. If you are going to build something that will have a profound impact on your family, your community and the world you live in, you are going to need the right tools for the job.

In this chapter I will fill your one small yes toolbox with useful tools, so you can pursue your calling without losing your mind and so you can stop falling for the lie that you can balance it all at once. I will show you the importance of having someone to keep you grounded and how to prune the nonsense out of your life so that you can focus on saying yes to what you have identified as important to you.

## Getting it all Done Without Losing Your Mind

It was just a few days past the spring recital in one of the early years of my business. My husband and I were walking through Sam's Club with our one-year-old in tow. I remember walking slowly through the electronics aisle while my daughter babbled and pointed at all of the shiny objects. On the outside we probably looked like a regular family out for an afternoon of shopping. My husband was saying something about the various sizes of flat screen TVs, but in my head a completely different conversation was taking place, and it went something like this: "I am going to lose my mind. Right here in the middle of Sam's Club."

To give you a bit of context, I had just survived my third year of recitals, auditions, class placements and registration—a two-week marathon of serving our families and responding to questions, and complaints, around the clock. I worked hard to keep up with emails while my daughter watched Elmo in the morning and tried to take care of important calls during her afternoon nap. Sleep was low and emotions were high. I couldn't go on this way anymore. As I watched my daughter happily play with something in the cart at Sam's Club that day, I tried desperately to convince myself I was going to be OK.

I did make it home that afternoon but not through the night. I finally broke, admitting to my husband I simply could NOT get everything done. I was trying to be a full-time, stay-at-home mom, a full-time entrepreneur and a full-time dance teacher, and I didn't feel like I was doing a good job at any of the roles. With my head in my hands and tears on my cheeks I entertained the idea of giving up on my calling and closing the doors forever. My husband, being the sweet, logical person that he is, listened patiently and then sent me to bed.

With some sleep under my belt, I was able to sit down with him the next day and have a productive conversation. Of course I did not want to give up on my calling! That was the last thing I wanted to do, but I didn't want to lose my family or my mind either. Something had to give—and that something was my irrational expectation that I needed to be, or even could be, everything to everybody all of the time.

And so the first tool had been added to my one small yes toolbox:

## Tool #1: Lower your expectations

Lower your expectations? If you're honest, that's probably not what you expected to hear as my number one tip for pursuing your calling and accomplishing big things one small yes at a time.

But, actually, it fits perfectly.

You see when I said one small yes to open my dance studio and let the classroom be my stage, I considered following my calling a black-and-white, yes-or-no proposition. There was no room for any gray area in the pursuit of the dream. But at some point my desire to do the very best job I could for every child and class went beyond a healthy discipline and focus. I wasn't chasing high expectations anymore, I was chasing perfection. And in doing so I had created an impossible situation for myself and my family.

My husband's advice to lower my expectations was the best lifeline I could have been given in that dark time. I realized that I wasn't going to be able to please everybody all of the time, so I gave myself permission to drop the impossible goal of a 100 percent approval rating. After all, if the president of the United States can barely crack the 50 percent margin most years, I could learn to be happy that 90 percent of my clients appreciated how I ran my business and my desire to make a difference with it.

I also lowered my expectation that I would be able to always know what the right decision should be every time. Business is not science. Business is people and relationships—and that takes some navigating. I accepted the fact that I wasn't always going to be able to be on-site at the business if I wanted to have a solid home life. I resigned myself to the truth that I wasn't going to be able to do everything for my family by myself at home if I wanted to run a business. This meant I would need help on both fronts, and I would need to trust other people to make decisions in my absence.

If I hadn't lowered my impossible expectations I most certainly would've folded under the pressure of perfection. My family would have suffered if I had kept the business going under my impossible expectations, and thousands of local children and hundreds of thousands of dancers worldwide would have missed out on healthier dance experiences if I had closed the business. Bringing my expectations into perspective so many years ago has allowed me to pursue my calling over the long term without losing my family or my mind.

## The Balancing Act Lie

In 2013, famed aerialist Nik Wallenda attempted the first televised Grand Canyon tightrope walk in history. Even though I knew there was a 10-second delay on the live broadcast in case something went tragically wrong, I still couldn't manage to watch the show with both eyes open. My hands were over my face, but I could see that Nik had made it partway across the thin line when he started to experience some reverberations. As the wind kicked up in the canyon, the waves in the line grew stronger, forcing Nik to hunker down in order to regain his balance. After several more starts and stops, and a few moments where it looked like he might not make it to the other side, Nik completed his daring quest as audiences across the country cheered from the safety of their living rooms.

As I watched that broadcast I had two different thoughts going through my head. One part of me was fascinated by this daring superhero who willingly put his life on the line to fulfill his calling to carry on his grandfather's legacy of aerial feats. The other part of me couldn't help but to find similarities between tightrope walking and entrepreneurship– the path I had chosen to fulfill MY calling. In entrepreneurship, like tightrope walking, the goal is far away, the risks are real, and there are times when the very best thing you can do is hunker down and wait for the waves and the wind to stop before you start again.

I'm not the first person to make this observation. I've heard it said many times that having a career and running a home is a balancing act. It's a statement that made a lot of sense to me as I started following my calling and growing my family. As my business grew and my family grew, I developed what I thought was a simple "balance strategy." I thought if I could divide my time and energy into enough small pieces I could parcel them out equally between the two areas of my life.

But that was not possible.

What I came to realize over time was that nobody wanted just a small piece of me and I didn't feel complete giving only part of myself to each of the important areas of my life. By the time our fourth child was born, the charade of the balancing act was over. It was simply not possible to balance work from home or to bring my home into the workplace any more. It was time to give up the mythical balancing act and learn to become comfortable being OFF-BALANCE, which leads me to the second tool in the one small yes toolbox.

**Tool #2: Get comfortable being off-balance**

I stopped imagining the relationship between my home and my work as a nervous tightrope walk and replaced that imagery with the sense of being on a teeter-totter—the kind you would find in an old school park. You might be up, or you might be down, but you can only be on one side at a time. I hired someone a few mornings a week to take care of the little ones at home so I could be present when I was at the studio. When I got home, I tried to discipline myself to turn off messages so I could engage with the family.

But even with the extra help at home and better boundaries regarding work, I was still divided into too many pieces. When my fifth child arrived, I knew it was time to take my comfort with being off-balance up another notch. I decided to take myself off of the regular teaching schedule to be home with my kids at night. This might not sound like a big change, but I had been in a dance studio almost every night of the week since I was a middle school student. My entire business was built on offering services in the evening, and I wasn't going to be there to deliver those services. Still, the change was necessary because I didn't want to miss out on our kids' growing-up years and activities.

The decision was a hard one both emotionally and economically. I had to remind myself that I wasn't giving up on my calling—to have a positive impact on children—just because somebody else would be teaching the classes. When clients or colleagues questioned my decision, I would answer, "I can always make up another dance or get paid for another class, but I'll never get a second chance to raise my children." I said yes to putting my calling on the shelf while I pursued the most important work I could do at the time: raising my kids.

The change left me feeling lonely at times and off-balance most of the time, but I was at peace knowing I was following the best yes for my life and for that season. With a capable team in place to run the daily operations of the business, I spent a year squarely in the off-balance position. I still had regular contact and responsibility with my studio, but my evenings were spent taking care of my own children and my days were open to other pursuits for the first time. I wrote articles for magazines, spoke at various events and took calls from other studio owners who struggled with the same things I had struggled with in the early years of my business –the weight of impossible expectations and the unachievable balancing act.

With a little more time on my hands, my mind started to wonder if what we had built locally, and the story of following my calling one small yes at a time, could somehow help other studio owners around the country follow their callings as well. For 18 months I dreamed about how I could translate the lessons I had learned, and the resources I had created, into something that would help others. That was when the idea for More Than Just Great Dancing® Affiliated Studios was born.

I firmly believe that if I had not gotten comfortable being off-balance, I would still be carefully dividing small pieces of myself between home and the studio; and I would never have found the space that I had needed to create More Than Just Great Dancing® Affiliated Studios.

Another very important thing happened when I took myself off of the evening teaching schedule to be home with the kids. I equipped other people to manage things at the studio for me when I wasn't there. One of those people was a long-term employee named Shayna.

## Kites and Strings

I met Shayna when she was a 10-year-old student in the weekly jazz class I taught at the studio where I had grown up dancing. Shayna and I had a great student-teacher relationship and she studied with me all the way through high school. Eventually Shayna became a teacher on my team at another studio before she left for college. Shayna had been a gifted teacher even in her teen years and I was sad to see her go.

When I said yes to my calling to be a teacher and start a dance studio, Shayna was one of the first people I called to share my big idea. She hopped on board enthusiastically and has been a part of the Misty's Dance Unlimited team for 18 of the 19 years we have been in business. The growth that she has shown from part-time teacher to administrative director and now to school director has been amazing to watch. Shayna is now what I affectionately call the "glue" of the school. She and I have also become business partners on two other ventures, including a retail store and a dance competition.

But Shayna is more than just the glue holding my studio operations together; she is the string to what has become the kite called the More Than Just Great Dancing® movement worldwide. The entire operation, which as of this writing is positively affecting more than 60,000 kids each week by way of our 164 Affiliated Studios, stands on the shoulders of what we do at our local studio each week. What we do at the local studio is Shayna's responsibility, which leads me to my third tool in the one small yes toolbox.

## Tool #3: Have a string for your kite

If I were a kite left to my own blue-sky thinking and entrepreneurial short attention span, I would either spend my day being whipped by the wind of my own ideas or getting stuck in a tree. There are literally no bounds to the things that I dream up on any given day. The folks on my leadership team would agree that it would be very rare to finish one of our weekly meetings without hearing me say the words, "So I have an idea!" Some of the ideas, such as More Than Just Great Dancing®, have turned out very well. But there have been as many, if not more, that have not (think second location).

Ideas are great, and ideation is a necessary part of growth. But keeping things in proper perspective with the big picture is critical. Shayna is the string to my studio kite. She helps me to measure my ideas against time, staff, cost and results. She keeps my kite from blowing away and makes sure that all the details of what we commit to launch are accounted for before we begin.

Liz is another important string in my life who has held four different positions within our family of companies. Because of that experience she has seen the true range of the benefits and challenges of my kite-thinking tendencies. In each of her roles she has been a grounding string-force for my own good.

When she worked as business manager at my dance studio, she brought order to the many new programs we were adding at the time with software and systems. As director of member care for More Than Just Great Dancing® she helped me create initiatives that made an actual difference for our members, not just more work for the team. In her current role as editorial director of our online magazine—a project she spearheaded—she keeps me focused on the purpose of our magazine when I want to run after new strategies by asking, "What is your vision this magazine?"

Liz still teaches classes at the dance studio, takes on extra lessons and mentors students on her own time. Through it all she continues to ask, "Does this decision, dance, program or article, help students become more confident for life?" As our companies have grown, Liz's influence has kept me on course with my calling time after time.

My sister, Alana, who now works full-time as director of operations for my dance-related businesses, is another string in my life, keeping me in check with my calling. Earlier this year I announced to her that I was going to start a podcast. I had a good friend I could hire to teach me the ropes and other friends who were already doing it successfully. I felt that I was behind the pack and was convinced we had to find time to start this new podcast. On my way out the door to a meeting, I stopped in her office to show her a proof of an intro for the podcast that was scheduled to be recorded by a professional company later that day. My instructions to her were rushed, but very clear:

> "I need you to shape this up so it can get sent to the recording studio this afternoon. It's only three sentences, but I don't have time to do it."
>
> Then she hit me with a truth bomb.
>
> "Misty, if you don't have time to rework three sentences, you don't have time to do a podcast."

Bam. String activated. Kite saved from being stuck in a tree–again. I emailed my friend and told him to put the podcast on hold. I didn't know if a podcast was a right thing for me anymore, but I was certain that it was not a "right now" thing.

If I had pursued that podcast I would have had to take my hands off of our studio affiliation program, which would've reduced the resources available for our new online student magazine. Had Alana not been the string to my kite that day, two businesses I care very much about would be hurting and I would be struggling to build a podcast audience at the same time. You've heard of the phrase "win-win"? Well left to my own ideas, this situation would've been lose-lose.

The grounding power of having a string for the kite of your calling cannot be overestimated. If you are going to stay on track with your true calling and make the impact on the world that you were designed to make, you are going to need a string for that kite of yours. Or in my case, maybe three.

## Socks and Rocks

Imagine this scene with me. It's 5 p.m. and your kids are hungry. In fact, they are more than hungry children; they are wild wolves opening cupboard doors looking for chips while you attempt to cook a hot meal.

One child is hanging on your leg while another is hanging from the ceiling fan. All they want and need right now is FOOD. And then in the middle of the chaos, you turn off the stove, shake the crying child off of your leg and dedicate yourself to picking up the stray socks in the living room.

Are you kidding me?

The kids are going out of their minds because it's dinnertime and you are going to stop making dinner and take care of the sock situation in the next room? No, you're not going to do that. Of course you aren't. You are going to turn the burner on the mac-n-cheese up higher and scoop some orange noodles (aka "silence") onto those plates as fast as you possibly can, which leads me to the fourth tool in the one small yes toolbox.

## Tool #4: Work on the big rocks, not the socks

Let's revisit the dinnertime example. Dinner is an immovable, "big rock" issue, every day of the week, whether you have children in your home or not. I know full well that everybody needs to eat after work and school, but I spent years being surprised that another evening had rolled around and I was facing frozen chicken at 5 p.m.

Serving "brinner" (breakfast for dinner) at my house wasn't a treat; it was a regular survival strategy to get some protein into the kids without having to make an actual meal. Because when the kids were losing their minds at dinnertime, the only thing I had on my mind was, "How can I stop this meltdown as fast as possible?"

Now apply the dinner situation to the pursuit of your calling. You are going to have big rock issues in your path every day. Are you going to tackle them head on or are you going to default to picking up socks in order to avoid doing the real work that needs to be done right now?

I have big rocks in the path to my calling, too. You've probably caught on by now that the scope of my calling has expanded over time.

What started with a small yes to open a dance studio instead of pursuing a performing career has now grown into training other studio owners and reaching dance students worldwide. The path I took from small-town studio owner to global influencer has included some amazing speaking opportunities around the world and many requests that I write a book about the one small yes story.

Writing this book has been a big rock in my life now for about a year. I started; then I stopped. I changed topics and then started again—and stopped again. I had forgotten my own one small yes tool: Work on the big rocks, not the socks. Somehow a whole year had passed and the big rock of the book was still sitting there quietly waiting for attention. Disgusted, but not surprised by my lack of progress on my biggest-rock goal of the year, I joined a book-writing program to hold my own feet to the fire.

I'm halfway through writing this book because I stopped picking up the socks in my life (email, social media, small problems, excuses and even laundry) long enough to put in the necessary time and effort to get this big rock rolling. And guess what I found once I got started in earnest? The first efforts were arduous—painful really. I faced self-doubt and was overwhelmed by the level of commitment required to write a book. I didn't know if I had it in me and I knew there were other things that needed attention (socks don't organize themselves after all, do they?).

But as I kept pushing the book rock an amazing thing happened—it started to become a little easier. I found a groove for the work, momentum kicked in and I started to enjoy telling the stories of my one small yes journey. I am predicting the second half of the book will be easier and more enjoyable to write than the first.

If I hadn't joined the book-writing program, I would probably still be picking up the unfinished outline every three weeks so that I could dust the table underneath it. If you are going to travel all the paths of your calling, you, too, are going to need to stop picking up the socks and start moving the big rocks.

But just as certain situations call for moving big rocks in your life, others call for moving them out of your life.

## Priorities and Pruning

I was seated expectantly on the right hand side of the conference table at the first of four High Performance Elite forums for CEOs produced by my mentor, Darren Hardy. I had recently graduated from the first two events so I knew that the bar would be set even higher for the 24 people chosen to attend the elite round.

Each attendee had been invited to share an eight-minute presentation about the greatest lesson they had learned in business. I was READY. I had prepared a compelling PowerPoint about my topic and brought custom cookies printed with each CEO's logo to reinforce the point of my presentation; that brand is everything their clients can consume. I even had a little ballerina cued to enter with the cookies at the six-minute point. It was a Super Bowl moment for me that went off without a hitch—a performance that our group still talks about to this day.

But it wasn't the most high-impact performance of the day. That presentation was much simpler. Marc was the first speaker to take the floor. He had no notes and nothing to put on the screen. But he did walk around the room and put a two-inch California Raisin® figurine in front of each attendee. We giggled a bit and turned the wrinkly plastic figures around in our hands while waiting for an explanation.

Marc's story was short. He told us how in spite of all his business success, he had gotten to a place where he wasn't enjoying life. He didn't feel well and he didn't sleep well, but no doctor could diagnose his malaise. So Marc came up with his own prescription: prune everything in his life that didn't give him joy or add to his sense of purpose. He pruned closets, garages, commitments and calendars. He sold off businesses, houses and vehicles. If it wasn't being used purposefully, it had to go no matter what it was. At the end of his short speech he simply said, "I gave you the raisins to remind you to always be pruning your life." Marc's speech leads me to the fifth tool in the one small yes toolbox.

## Tool #5: Always be pruning

After hearing Marc's message I became interested to learn more about the concept of pruning. The great Wiki lists the following as some of the reasons for pruning plants:

- Deadwood removal
- Controlling or directing growth
- Improving or maintaining health
- Preparing specimens for transplanting
- Increasing yield or quality of fruit
- Removal of diseased, damaged or nonproductive tissue

Any horticulturist will tell you that regular pruning is vital to a plant's health and eventual fruit. Likewise, regular pruning of your activities and "stuff" is vital to your ability to continue to say yes to your calling and produce results. From your calendar to your closet, from your checkbook to the books on your shelves, from your commitments to your relationships and from your physical space to your mental space, regular pruning will make your calling grow stronger and faster, while yielding greater results.

Our group has done a lot of reminiscing about my ballerina presentation over the past few years, but we've acted a lot more on Marc's pruning message. I have radically pruned my home, my calendar and my projects, and in the process made room for more small yes decisions towards my big calling. With less physical and emotional clutter in my life, it's easier to show up for the things that matter to me most. If you are going to keep focused on your calling, you, too, will need to prune any distractions that might keep you from running the race you were meant to run.

## Showing up for Your Life

I met Melanie and her partner Jo-D while I was teaching at a business conference. Actually, it would be a stretch to say that I "met" them—I was teaching about employee benefits from the main stage, when Jo-D shouted out, "How about I come work for you?" I recognized her in the hotel café later that day and we exchanged pleasantries and contact information. I had no idea that day what a deep and meaningful friendship we would develop in the years to come.

Over the course of the months following the conference, Melanie and I kept in touch by email. I could tell that she had a sharp mind for business and a real passion to make a difference in the lives of her students. When I said yes to the next step of my calling by forming More Than Just Great Dancing® Affiliated Studios, Melanie and Jo-D were among the first people I told. I can remember sitting in their living room sharing my vision. I don't know how well I articulated my ideas that day, but I shared enough about my journey as a studio owner and my idea for other studio owners to follow their *own* callings with confidence that they jumped on board.

Melanie was a quick study and an active member of our community that we affectionately called "The Tribe" from the very first day we launched. She has attended many of our live events and contributed frequently to our member forums. Recently she was recognized by her peers as member of the year and then donated her prize to another member who was struggling financially. She launched a chapter of the National Society for Dance Arts and then trained other affiliate schools to do the same. She has doubled the size of her business and expanded the reach of her programs to a second location. She is currently in the process of forming a nonprofit organization to provide more charitable giving opportunities for her students and her community.

Melanie is a picture of progress in every sense of the word. She could easily sit back, go on autopilot and enjoy the ride. But she doesn't. She comes to our signature event, Studio Owner University®, every year. She attends teleseminars, webinars and trainings; she asks questions and shares insights. Melanie is the living example of the sixth tool in the one small yes toolbox.

## Tool #6: Never stop learning

Melanie has experienced some amazing successes, but that doesn't mean that the wins have come easily. Melanie would be the first to tell you that she'd rather read a book than work on QuickBooks and that she's more comfortable picking up the socks than moving the big rocks. She has had to learn to hire for her weaknesses in order to amplify her strengths. She would still rather do something fast herself than take the time to teach someone else how to do it. And yes, there are days when doubt still creeps in at the edges of her resolve to follow her calling. Melanie is a super-achiever, but she is also human. She never stops learning how to say yes to her calling in better and smarter ways.

The important lesson here is that you can embrace your calling without losing your mind and you don't have to divide yourself into a million pieces to do it. Stay close to people who keep you grounded and learn how to prune the nonsense out of your life so you can focus on saying yes to building a life and business that make a difference. The rocks won't move themselves so keep learning the tools that will help you to move them better. As my dad would say, "You have to have the right tools for the job."

*Chapter 5*

# The Unconventional Yes

un·con·ven·tion·al
ˌənkənˈven(t)SH(ə)n(ə)l/
*adjective:* (not based on or conforming
to what is generally done or believed)

The world is filled with people who live logical lives. But I have the feeling that if you are reading this book you are not one of them. You have a calling, a mark to make on the world. Following that calling is going to take sacrifice and a willingness to make unconventional decisions.

At times this will make you will feel like a square peg in a round hole, but you will eventually become comfortable with—well, with being uncomfortable. You don't need to conform to what is generally done or believed. You are capable of making the unconventional yes decisions that are necessary to live the life that you want to live. It won't be easy, but with grace and grit, you can do it one small yes at a time.

In this chapter we will explore reasons for the "unconventional yes" along with some stories of people who have gone against entire industries and left careers to follow their callings. I will also share how the fleeting nature of time should influence your yes decisions and how you can make something meaningful out of the ingredients you've been given in life. If you've ever felt like your calling is a little unorthodox, this chapter was written for you.

## Square-Peg, Round-Hole Living

I met Leslie Scott through a mutual acquaintance a year ago. In the span of one phone call, I was convinced I was talking to a woman on a mission. Leslie's calling is enormous–to change the way the world sees dance by educating an entire industry about the dangers of hyper-sexualization and objectification of kids in dance. And she is doing it one workshop, one video, one conversation and one small yes at a time.

Leslie started her career in dance with the intention to use the art form for social justice, community building and inclusiveness. That changed when she moved to Hollywood and admittedly was consumed by the pursuit of fame and status. Leslie performed and taught on the professional circuit for years before she started slowly becoming aware of the increasingly damaging messages that many children were being exposed to. The movements students were being taught to perform, the adult costuming they were being told to wear and music messages they were being forced to listen to over and over again in their dance experiences was taking a toll.

As the evidence mounted–and she saw more and more students each year suffering from self-image issues–Leslie became convinced of her calling to become an advocate for healthy experiences in dance. Leslie didn't know what this new journey would look like but made the decision to stop being part of the problem and start being part of the solution. She had no idea how one person could change an entire industry, but she said an unconventional yes to walk away from her former life as an industry dancer and start a nonprofit organization called Youth Protection Advocates in Dance, or YPAD for short.

My conversation with Leslie that day was so compelling that I offered to fly her, her husband, her child and her assistant to our offices and to become the first "Visionary Sponsor" of their work. In the course of the week we spent together, I learned about the great strides she has made and the many struggles she has faced since changing the focus of her work from entertainment to advocacy.

On one hand, Leslie has accomplished more as a lone, but passionate voice to raise awareness of these issues than any of the dominant businesses in the industry. She has even earned the support of influencers such as Dr. Tomi Ann Roberts of the American Psychological Association's Task Force on the Sexualization of Girls.

The other side of the coin is that Leslie has paid a deep and personal price for her willingness to be a square peg to the industry's round hole, losing friends, agents and job opportunities along the way. The road has not been easy, but Leslie carries on with her unconventional yes. She is OK with the high price tag she has paid to be different because there is no price on a child's sense of self-worth.

Leslie is changing an entire industry because she gave an unconventional yes to become a dance activist. Your calling may not be as controversial as Leslie's, but at some point in your journey, you, too, will have to say yes to something unconventional. You will also have to be OK not conforming to something that is generally believed or done. You can't change the world by being like it. If you are going to build a life and business that make a difference, you, too, are going to have to become comfortable with the fact that your unconventional choices might make you misunderstood among your family, peers and colleagues.

## Get Comfortable Being Misunderstood

Austin Kleon is the *New York Times* bestselling author of three illustrated books: *Steal Like An Artist, Newspaper Blackout* and *Show Your Work!* Austin calls himself a writer who draws, who pursues creativity in the digital age. His work has been translated into 20 languages and his message has been shared with such organizations as Pixar, Google, SXSW and TEDx.

Although his work is widely circulated and influential, that doesn't mean it has always been understood. Austin has been quoted as saying, "People will misinterpret you and what you do. So get comfortable with being misunderstood, disparaged or ignored–the trick is to be 'too busy doing your work to care.'" That is great wisdom for people who want to spend their lives doing work that matters.

If you have ever felt misunderstood while following your calling, you are in good company. Shanna, a client of mine, had to press through a lot of disbelief in order to build a new building for her business. Despite getting a lot of noes from others, she kept saying yes to herself. She knew she was ready to take the leap to build her facility because she was confident, beyond any doubt, that she had been called to do so. The banker's answer? "Just enjoy where your hobby has gotten you so far, and focus on raising your children instead of your business." Some people might have crumbled at those words, but it made Shanna's focus on her goal that much more intense.

Shanna wouldn't let the disparaging remarks take her eyes off the prize of that building she felt called to build. Finally, she got three yeses that changed her life: an amazing bank that believed in her and two friends who put money into CDs as extra collateral while the building was being built. Those friends not only helped change the course of her business forever, but also helped her touch the lives of 1,000 kids who have taken lessons in that building over the past three years.

Whether you are established in your work like Austin, or you have just said your first yes to the journey ahead like Shanna, get comfortable with the idea of being misunderstood. Not everybody is going to see what you have been called to do as clearly as you do. In fact, they are more likely to not see it, cut it down or ignore it all together than they ever would be to comprehend it, cheer it on or pay much attention to it. Some of these people might be ugly at heart, but most of them are simply too busy building their own lives and pursuing their own callings to try to understand yours. Keep saying yes anyway, even if it is unconventional to the people around you. The world needs you to do what you have been called to do and make the mark you were made to make. You don't have time to waste.

## Zenosyne

Time is a funny thing. "Zenosyne"–the sense that time keeps going faster–is an invented word by John Koenig, the author of *The Dictionary of Obscure Sorrows*. The word may be made up, but I think you'll agree with me that the definition describes a real experience.

When my first daughter was born I remember being annoyed by the little old ladies who would stop me in the parking lot at Target to tell me to enjoy every moment because it would go so fast. Enjoy every moment? I couldn't say that I exactly enjoyed getting up every two hours all night or the nervousness that accompanied taking care of her during her first fever. "You come enjoy every moment while I go take a nap," I thought crabbily to myself.

That same daughter, at the time of this publication, just finished her freshman year of high school. Oh, how I wish I could take back those overtired, crabby thoughts. The activities that used to seem endless are now on countdown. Just yesterday I was driving her to an audition and she said, "Mom! Do you realize I only have three more auditions left for the ballet before I graduate?" I choked out a correction, "Actually you only have two more. The one you are doing today is for your production you will do during your sophomore year. All you'll have left after this is your junior and senior year audition."

*"Life is short. And life is long. But not in that order."*
**– John Koenig**

The phenomenon of zenosyne has caused me to make some unconventional yes decisions. When my children were babies, I looked forward to a nightly break from parenting and spending time teaching classes with my students. But as my children grew, I understood that I was exchanging the decreasing amount of time I had to raise my own kids for spending my evenings making memories with other people's children. At the height of my teaching career, zenosyne caused me rethink the hours I was spending in the studio.

Sometimes the sense that time keeps going faster causes me to slow down and appreciate the moment. Other times it causes me to hurry up because time is running out. For example, when I was a child I worked with my dad to remodel our houseboat. Many of the best memories I have growing up are tied to making trips to the hardware store with my dad and listening to the radio in the boat while we worked to carve functional areas out of the small space.

When the recent tiny house movement started gaining national attention, I wondered what it would be like to revisit those early building years with my dad and work on another project together. After my dad spent some time in the hospital this year I talked more and more about the potential project, but I still had not done anything to make it happen. Then one day I walked out of my office and saw that my husband had left a tiny house trailer in the parking lot with a bow on it. There was no card, but the message was clear to me: Get going!

My unconventional yes to step away from regular teaching has allowed me to make many rich memories of ordinary life with my kids. I am hoping my unconventional yes to build a tiny house will create opportunities to make more memories with my dad.

The sense that time keeps going faster will cause you to make unconventional yes decisions as well. Whether you say yes to slowing down when most people would expect you to be ramping up or you say yes to starting something now because you feel you are running out of time, it's good to let the value of time weigh in on what you say yes to each day.

## Above the Cloud

In 1972 the real estate industry was a locally owned business model dominated by college-educated, white, middle-aged, middle-class men, and the Van Schaak brand was the epitome of that reputation. Dave Liniger, a recent college dropout with a wife and three children, had none of the polish or experience of the other agents at Van Schaack where he worked, but he was excellent at selling real estate.

After achieving some success selling, Dave came to believe that agents would work harder if they received a greater benefit from their time and effort. He approached his boss with the revolutionary idea of creating a new system where agents would keep 100% of their commissions in return for a monthly fee. His belief was that every agent in the world would want to work for such a firm. He was absolutely convinced that tying a reward system like this to a strong brand like the firm would revolutionize the industry.

And revolutionize the industry it most certainly did! But not at Van Schaack. Dave's boss took a pass on the opportunity and today 100,000-plus real estate agents, in 96 countries keep 100 percent of their commission–as part of the RE/MAX team, not Van Schaak. Van Who? Exactly.

The RE/MAX story isn't unconventional just because of a commission shift. Creating an environment where everybody wins was at the core of Dave's many unconventional yes decisions. He said yes to hiring women and minorities, something that wasn't common in the industry. And he empowered agents to build their own offices; putting their name front and center on every RE/MAX branded promotional piece–another idea that was fiercely resisted by the industry. He also said yes to franchising, a model that had been previously unproven in real estate, but one that gave the RE/MAX brand an unparalleled opportunity to grow and its broker owners an unlimited opportunity to earn and grow.

The path to success was a difficult one but it was built on an unwavering dedication to the dream and cowboy bravado. There were many obstacles along the way, including personal tragedy, industry dives and economic fluctuations, but an unconventional yes attitude overcame each adversity, providing Dave and his team an opportunity to grow stronger with every challenge.

One of Dave's most recent challenges was recovering from an eight-month coma caused by a staph infection that left him quadriplegic. When I met Dave he was a little over a year into his rehabilitation. He opened the session at the forum we were both attending by asking the group to stand up–and then sit down. He followed the attention-grabbing introduction by saying, "If you can do that, you are among the wealthiest people in the world." For all of Dave's financial success, he carries an understanding that real wealth is having your health and people to share life with.

And sharing is something that Dave does very well. Today RE/MAX is a publicly traded company whose charitable contributions include raising more than $130 million for Children's Miracle Network

Hospitals. They have also opened their acclaimed private golf course, The Sanctuary, for charity events which have in turn raised $60 million for hundreds of organizations since opening in 1997.

Dave's one small yes to his vision more than 40 years ago, and all the unconventional yes decisions he made while building RE/MAX, have made him a legend in the industry and a giant in my life personally.

Don't get over-wowed or discouraged by the big numbers in this story. The same truth that applies to Dave's journey applies to you: If you want to build a business that makes a difference, you must raise your thinking above the cloud of the ordinary. Be prepared for your idea to be dismissed by others. That isn't meant to be a discouragement. Being rejected serves a purpose: it affirms your calling and it gets you prepared for the unconventional yes.

## Same Ingredients, Different Outcomes

Here is an interesting exercise. Look closely at the following ingredient list:

- Flour
- Baking powder
- Salt
- Sugar
- Egg
- Oil
- Water

Can you guess what I'm making? Pancakes? Maybe. Pizza crust? Possibly.

It depends on how you put the ingredients together. The same ingredients in different ratios can yield completely different results. Go heavier on the egg, baking soda and sugar and you have breakfast on your hands. Reduce the water and baking soda and brush the egg on top and you have the base for dinner. The same ingredients can be pancakes by morning, pizza crust by night.

Life has some similarities to baking. Although we all come from different backgrounds and circumstances, we all have the same ingredients to work with: time, energy, talent, intellect, resources and opportunities. Some have more of one thing than another, but something can be made out of those six ingredients no matter how much you have of each. So why do some people make masterpieces with their ingredients while others make a mess out of theirs? I believe it has something to do with the unconventional yes.

Wes Moore wrote about this in his widely praised book, *The Other Wes Moore: One Name, Two Fates*. The author had been lauded by his hometown newspaper for becoming the first African-American graduate of Johns Hopkins to become a Rhodes Scholar. That very same day another man by the name of Wes Moore was in the newspaper for the murder trial of a police officer, something that haunted the author for years. The author eventually wrote to the other Wes Moore and their correspondence became the basis for his book.

The two men had many of the same ingredients in their background including growing up fatherless and getting into trouble in school. But there came a point when the author stopped following the path prescribed to him by circumstances and started following the higher expectation set for him by his family, teachers and peers–this unconventional turn compounded in positive ways over time, until he had a completely different fate from the other Wes Moore.

You might not have the same life ingredients that the Wes Moores had, but you have the same opportunity to defy any circumstance. Unconventional yes thinking–the ability to see beyond what circumstance says is probable–will help you see what's possible to create with the ingredients you've been given.

## When Your Calling is...Strange

Much of what I love about the one small yes journey is that so much of it is just plain common sense with a better logo. After all, there is nothing overtly strange about spending time to consider what your unique contribution in this world is and then beginning your way toward that calling one small yes at a time. In fact, I might argue that it would be strange NOT to consider why you are here or and strange not to want to do anything about it.

Think about what I've shared already in this book, teaching you how to fight distractions, work on best yes activities and develop routines. I've also showed you that you need to put what you learn into practice, eat the live frog first, get a string for your kite-like ways and rest when you're tired. It all makes logical sense. Blame it on my hearty Midwest background or my grandpa's Norwegian practicality, but I'm a fan of doing things that just make sense.

But what if the thing you think you are supposed to do in this life is something that doesn't make sense? What if what you feel called to do isn't on a career chart or makes the people around you a bit uncomfortable? Then trigger the unconventional yes and keep going anyway.

Your calling isn't being graded on some kind of imaginary curve of all callings. Your calling is not assigned a better value if it earns more money than my calling, and my calling doesn't get a better score if it reaches more people than your calling. The worth of your calling isn't measured by how much money it makes, how much praise it receives, how many followers it accumulates or how glamorous the destination. Jesus, arguably among the most influential figures of all history, had no money, was hated by his contemporaries and lost almost every follower when his calling was fulfilled by hanging on a tree.

Friend, if you are confident that you have been called to do something really hard—something so unconventional that it makes your friends and family wonder at your sanity—you are going to have to lean into the unconventional yes to get the job done. I know some people who have done just that and their stories inspire me every day.

My husband, Mitch, is one those people. A technology education teacher by trade, he visited Cite Soleil, Haiti, on a trip of mutual exchange in 2011. One of the purposes of the trip was to raise support for a school in an area that Mother Teresa once called the poorest slum in the Western Hemisphere. Everybody he was travelling with that day saw the children inside the school, but my husband's eyes were fixed on the young men outside the gate.

While he agreed that supporting the academic school was a worthy idea, and even signed on to be a sponsor of several students, he understood that for most of the students in that plywood-and-tarp school, there would be no jobs waiting for them after graduation.

Mitch was invited to return to Haiti to build desks for the school to replace those that had been lost in the well-documented earthquake of 2010. He was able to build three desks by the end of his trip. He got an email from Haiti a week later with a picture showing that the men from outside the gate had built 23 more desks with the tools he had left behind. In that moment, Mitch knew he was being called to teach the men of the community to build their own future, not to do it for them.

Mitch returned to the island to provide training for the men in welding so that they could find work and rebuild their community. As the airline miles added up, the projects that the men tackled did, too–first desks, then benches, doors, rocking chairs and water filtration machines. They even handcrafted a giant arch above the broken street at the entrance to the community announcing a new vision for its people. Each project represented the men's best hopes for their community.

As much as Mitch enjoyed the trips, the pace of keeping up a full-time teaching job in the U.S. and a part-time teaching job in Haiti was not sustainable. Logic would have suggested he scale back on the overseas trips and keep the day job, but Mitch said an unconventional yes to quit his 15-year career as a teacher and start a 501(c)(3) called Global Groundwork. With five kids at home and a self-employed wife, the decision to walk away from the only steady paycheck and benefits he had ever known was not a light one, but it was the right one.

Had Mitch not said an unconventional yes to walking away from the security of teaching in America he wouldn't be doing what he is today, which is building a vocational school and community center right across the street from the plywood-and-tarp school where the men sat outside the gate so many years ago. Mitch said one small yes to build some desks and another yes to train those men to build not just desks, but their own futures. Today the young men in the program are finding jobs and starting small businesses because Mitch followed his calling.

Mitch's story is a reminder that it's OK if a calling might look a little strange to the world. It's OK to be a square peg in a round hole; in fact, that might be just what it takes to follow your calling. Get comfortable being misunderstood and be willing to say yes to yourself even when others say no. The unconventional yes is based on NOT conforming to what is generally done or believed.

## Chapter 6

# The Smallest Yes

*E*ven before I wrote a word of this book I knew that this chapter was going to be my favorite. The "smallest yes" has a special place in my heart because as a teen and young adult I felt like so many things were out of my reach, that what I wanted to do was simply too big for my experience, skills and resources. I didn't start with the smallest yes because it was logical or I thought it would become a book someday; I started that way because I didn't have any other options. I literally thought to myself, "I don't know if I can do all of this, but I can do SOMETHING so I might as well start."

I've since come to realize that the smallest yes can be the most powerful of all: yielding results exponentially greater than the original effort. Scientists call this the "butterfly effect," or the idea that something as large as a hurricane can be influenced by something as small as the flapping of a butterfly's wings. The smallest yes is the "butterfly effect" of the one small yes theory. Don't underestimate the influence of the smallest of yes decisions.

In this chapter I will show you how to fight the fear that your calling is too big and how to tackle it one small yes at a time. I will share with you how to grow a life and business that you love and how to avoid the death of a calling. You will understand the importance of developing a yes mindset and how measuring the miles as you go will keep you heading in the right direction. You will learn that regardless of the size of your calling you can get started, keep going and reach your destination, or beyond, with even the smallest of yeses.

## What if My Calling is Too Big?

You have probably wondered several times throughout the reading of this book if your calling is too big, too audacious or too far out of reach. Let me just put your fears to rest right now.

Of course, your calling is too big!

If your calling could fit into the size of your current abilities and experiences, it wouldn't be a calling; it would be a *circumstance*. It would be something that happened to you or that you happened upon, but not something that you made happen.

Your calling is simply not something you choose from a variety of options at the store and it's not something you put in your pocket as a reminder of all that you can be in this life. Your calling is a destination, something that you, and only you, were designed to do from the beginning of time. Imagine with me that the whole spectrum of time from beginning to end is a giant puzzle, and each of us is a specially shaped piece that helps to tell the story when completed. I don't carry the image of your piece, and your piece won't fit where my piece was meant to go. We all have a special piece of the puzzle of life.

You will encounter challenges on your journey, but be assured that even the smallest yes choices that you can manage now can have hurricane level effects in the future. If the random activity of a butterfly can have an impact on global weather conditions, purposeful and intentional small activity on your part will eventually have an impact on the mark you were meant to make in this world.

And that calling you think is so big right now? Wait, because good things become better things and small things lead to even bigger things. My original calling to open a dance studio seemed huge to me at the time—but it now seems small compared to my larger calling to train and equip dance studio owners all over the world. And I shouldn't have been surprised that once I felt confident leading my worldwide dance studio association that my calling expanded again to include serving students via an online magazine—a natural extension of our service to studio owners but something with which I had absolutely no experience.

When my calling expanded to reaching students through an online magazine, I once again found myself saying the smallest of yeses. I didn't know how to build such a site, but I knew I could spend two minutes on GoDaddy to register a domain name. That tiny yes to register a domain name led to a series of other larger yes decisions including hiring a writer, editor, graphic designer, photographer, public relations specialist, web developer and videographer to do the work I couldn't do myself but could see in my mind. Ten months after my smallest yes to do the only thing I knew how to do—register a domain name—the website had been visited by more than a half million people. If I hadn't said that smallest yes, all the people I hired wouldn't have had those jobs, and the inspiring content we created wouldn't have been seen by all of those young dancers.

My vision for what my businesses can be and do in the world is still expanding beyond my skill set and resources. I am again in a place where I don't know how to make the next part of the big picture vision come to life. I am relying on what has gotten me to where I am today–making the next yes decision, even if it seems like the smallest yes yet.

Whether your smallest yes is simply agreeing that there IS a calling in your life or making an official agreement on paper to start a business to pursue your calling, the smallest yes can be the first step towards making the mark you know you were created to make in this world. Don't let the size of your calling intimidate you; it's meant to motivate you to start saying yes to creating a life of meaning.

## How Do You Eat an Elephant?

You've probably heard this phrase before: "How do you eat an elephant? One bite at a time." I think the first time I heard this phrase was in elementary school. Although I couldn't imagine why anybody would want to eat an elephant, I understood the concept of breaking something big into small pieces.

Your calling is like that elephant–too big to be taken in one bite. You're not supposed to tackle your entire calling all at one time. In fact, that would be no fun at all. Can you imagine the letdown of working through this entire book, identifying your calling and then washing your hands of the completed work by dinnertime? If you could complete your calling in one sitting, it wouldn't be a calling or a journey; it would be an event. I don't know what mark you have been called to make in this world, but I do know that if you could get it done in one day, there would not be a lot of purpose to the rest of your days.

Your calling is a destination and the one small yes mind set is your vehicle to get there. Imagine I want to travel from where I live in Wisconsin to California. The most efficient way to get there is by airplane. If I choose that method of travel, in a matter of a few hours and a couple of connections I can exchange the Dairyland for Disneyland. But flying isn't the only way to get to California from where I live. If I didn't have the resources to fly, I could also take the train or drive my car.

I could even ride my bike or walk if I had to, it would just take a really, really long time and be a very difficult journey.

The idea of pursuing your calling may feel like making a trip from Wisconsin to California. If you have all the resources and skills you may be able to pull the trip off in a day. But if you look at your calling and feel totally resourced and equipped to accomplish it in a short period of time, I would seriously question whether or not you have identified your calling or just had an idea for a fun day trip.

I have never met a person who felt equipped to follow their calling when they started or who got the job done in one day. Every person I have ever met who has accomplished, or at least moved toward their calling, has felt overwhelmed and underprepared to do so. And still they said yes one step at a time.

You will follow your calling the same way. One small yes at a time—even if it's the smallest yes imaginable. But be assured that even a humble beginning is still a beginning. This is such an important truth to understand that I will say it again. Even a humble beginning is still a beginning! One of my favorite Bible verses is "Do not despise these small beginnings, for the Lord rejoices to see the work begin," Zechariah 4:10. It makes me smile to consider that God delights in my small beginnings. If a small beginning is no disappointment to the Creator then it shouldn't be a disappointment to you or me either.

## What You Feed Grows

There is a parable of unknown origin about an old Cherokee chief who was teaching his grandson about life. "A fight is going on inside of me," he said to the young boy. "It is a terrible fight and it is between two wolves. One is evil—he is anger, envy, sorrow, regret, greed, arrogance, self-pity, guilt, resentment, inferiority, lies, false pride, superiority, self-doubt and ego. The other is good—he is joy, peace, love, hope, serenity, humility, kindness, benevolence, empathy, generosity, truth, compassion and faith. This same fight is going on inside of you and every other person, too." The grandson thought about it for a minute and then asked his grandfather, which wolf will win? The old chief simply replied, "The one you feed."

That same fight is going on inside of you and me. It can be a fight between tying your identity to what you do instead of who you are. It can be a fight between seeing past mistakes as failures or as fuel for new beginnings. It's a fight between knowing what to do and actually putting your knowledge into action. It's a fight between defaulting to distraction-actions and spending time on high value activities. It's a fight between our nature to pick up socks and the need to move big rocks. It's a fight between knowing when to brake and when to accelerate. But most importantly it's a terrible fight between fear and saying even this smallest yes to your calling. To predict which one will win you need only to look to the old chief's reply: "The one you feed."

So which wolf will you feed? When you bought this book, you fed the good wolf. When you say yes to the first step of your calling, the good wolf gets fed again. If you are going to tackle that thing you think is too big right now it's important to understand that even the smallest yes you can muster still feeds the good wolf. And if you feed the good wolf enough, even with the smallest of yeses, it will eventually grow stronger.

But it's not just about the good wolf getting stronger. The other side of the story is that the bad wolf gets weaker if you stop feeding it. Wouldn't you love for your bad habits, fears and doubts to become weaker? You don't need a doctorate in behavioral health to beat those things into submission. You just need to stop feeding them.

This parable of the wolves reminds me of my dance training. As a high school student I was a generalist, taking an equal number of classes for each genre. I was strong but not excellent at any one style. In college I took a summer course at Harvard University and auditioned to be a part of a special jazz dance training opportunity there. By the end of the course, I moved like a jazz dancer. A few years later we had a vacancy in the tap department at my dance studio. So I fed the tap dancer inside of me and eventually became co-valedictorian of my graduating class at the American Tap Dance Institute. I wasn't naturally a strong tap dancer, but two years of focused time and attention created strength in an area I didn't have before. The same thing happened when I took a teacher training course in ballet and later developed an interest in yoga. Whatever I have focused my time and attention on throughout my dance career has become stronger, and whatever I have ignored has become weaker.

The human body responds to whatever you feed it, whether that is a certain type of physical activity or a certain type of food. It turns out Grandma was right all along–you are what you eat. Your mental life is exactly the same way–it will respond to what you feed it. When you feed your knowledge and starve your inadequacies, your skills will grow. When you feed the good wolf, your discipline, and starve the bad wolf, that negative self talk, your positive outcomes will grow. When you feed your faith muscles and starve your fear muscles, your confidence will grow. Commit to feed your mind the good stuff even if you can only manage the smallest yes at a time.

## Death by 1,000 Paper Cuts

A couple of years ago I was interviewing for the opportunity to attend an event called MasterMind Talks in Toronto. I understood I was the one being interviewed for one of the few coveted spots, nevertheless I couldn't help but turn the tables on the genius of a man who had built an event where ordinary people like me could network with some of the most famous entrepreneur success stories of our time.

Mastermind Talks was a relatively new venture so I asked Jayson, the founder, why he left his previous career at the very large online ticketing company he had built. Jayson's answer was candid and clear, "I built a business that I hated, which enabled me to buy things that I didn't need, to impress people that I didn't like. I ended up unconsciously sabotaging everything. There was no cataclysmic event at the end. It was death by 1,000 paper cuts."

If Jayson's first business ended by 1,000 paper cuts, his new business was given life via 1,000 small yes choices. Jayson didn't know what he would do with his life when he walked away from his first business, but he knew he wanted to say yes to a different kind of life and to building meaningful relationships with the people in his life. He had an innate curiosity, a calling, to serve and support a small group of individuals. Instead of investing in a business this time around, Jayson chose to invest in people. He had no resources and few connections but he took the smallest yes step toward this new vision for his life by inviting a group of successful business people to dinner to talk about the lessons of business. He paid for it all on his own even though he was hundreds of thousands of dollars in debt from his failed first venture.

That small dinner so many years ago was the first of many small yes decisions Jayson would make on the road to fulfilling his calling. Yes to another dinner. Yes to creating a dinner series. Yes to launching a live event. Yes to reaching out to the most famous entrepreneurs on earth to speak at his live event. Yes to starting a podcast and then yes to starting it again when the first one didn't work out. Yes to writing a best-selling book. And yes to selecting a small group of entrepreneurs to mentor on a regular basis—not to mention a thousand yes decisions in between. His life doesn't look anything like it did before, and for Jayson, that is the best part. He took the smallest yes of inviting some business people to dinner and built a life of opportunity for himself and others.

## Yes to "The Next Thing" Mindset

Recently I had an opportunity to hear Mark Owen, former Navy SEAL and best-selling author of *No Easy Day* and *No Hero*, share lessons on leadership at a private event. As I listened to him speak I recognized that this was a man who knew the importance of the smallest yes in a way that you and I could never understand as civilians. A week later I spent an hour on the phone with Mark. We talked about his early desire to become a SEAL, the 14 tours he spent serving our country and the well-publicized missions he had been involved with, including the rescue of Captain Phillips from the Maersk Alabama hijacking in 2009 and Operation Neptune Spear, which resulted in the death of Osama bin Laden in 2011.

Mark was quick to credit the small yes mindset he had acquired early in his Navy training for his ability to pursue his calling to serve his country as a SEAL. Mark said, "When you're in a bad situation, you just need a sliver of hope. That's what SEAL training was. They push you to the absolute limit and then right when it's so gnarly you don't think you can go on, they give you 20 minutes of sleep or a dry set of clothes."

BUD/S Training, the training required to become a Navy SEAL is known as the toughest military training in the world and has a 75-80 percent attrition rate. I asked Mark how he kept going knowing that only two or three soldiers out of every ten would complete the course. Mark replied, "I never once thought of quitting because I only thought about doing the next thing, not the whole thing. I just thought, 'I'm going to do all I can to recoup and get ready for the next challenge.' It's all a mindset."

You and I may not have the experience of SEAL training, but the benefit of the SEAL mindset is available to everyone simply by saying yes to the next thing. There will come a time when you are going to be pushed to the absolute limit and think that you can't go on. That's when you have to narrow your focus from that calling you think is too big and just give the smallest yes to the next thing. If you want to be one of the last men standing–one of those who doesn't bow out when your calling gets hard–follow Mark's example doing all you can to recoup between trainings and get ready for the next yes again and again.

## Measure the Miles

Last week my son Max asked me to go canoeing with him. The day was crisp and clear and we both needed the activity so I agreed to paddle about halfway down the island to the boat landing. After some initial splashing around, our oars found a steady, if not lop-sided, rhythm due to the difference in our sizes. We had been paddling for about ten minutes when I started to question my decision to make the boat landing our destination. The air that had been crisp and refreshing when we started was now cold against our legs, and our feet had become wet from the inefficient paddling. The sun was beginning to drop behind the bluffs and the boat landing was nowhere in sight. We kept paddling, but our confidence was starting to wane.

At one point I became convinced that it would be a better idea to turn around and head back instead of continuing to paddle with no end in sight. Before I announced the decision to Max, I decided to look back. I was shocked to see how far we had come in such a short time. I couldn't even see our house or the neighbor's house for that matter anymore. We had come too far to stop now. I didn't know exactly how close we were to our destination but seeing how far we had come from our starting place gave us the energy to keep going until we found the boat landing.

Following your calling is a lot like that canoe trip. There will be a time when you feel like giving up, but you will look back and realize that you've come too far to quit. When you aren't sure that you can make it to your destination, look back from time to time on your journey to measure your progress. Seeing how far you have come will give you a renewed sense of energy to finish what you started.

There is another valuable reason to look back and measure where you have been. Perhaps you've heard this maxim quoted by Dr. Phil on afternoon television: "The biggest predictor of future success is past behavior." Indeed there is something powerful about looking back to past successes to provide fuel for future yeses. When you are struggling to find the energy to make the next small yes decision, even if it is the smallest of yeses to keep moving forward, you will be encouraged by remembering other times when you were tired or doubtful but took the next step anyway.

You will always have fears that your calling is too big, but you can put fear in its place with the smallest yes. Focus on feeding the good wolf and understand the power of developing a yes mindset to keep going when you feel like giving up. Take care to measure the miles and track your progress as you work towards building the life of meaning that you were created to live. Remember: No calling is too big and no yes is too small.

## Chapter 7

# The Art of Yes is No

**W**ithout a doubt, I am an advocate of saying yes to your calling no matter how daily, small or unconventional the yes might be. Yes is the vehicle that will take you to the destination of your calling–that one special thing that you and you alone have been created to do in this world.

There are as many varieties of callings as there are people in the world. Regardless of what you have been called to do, your calling will be fueled by the series of small yes decisions you make each day, the culmination of which will eventually determine the course of your life.

But the one small yes journey is not just a checklist or a formula for saying yes. It is also an art–and the art of yes includes knowing when to say NO. No is the string to the yes-kite. There are pitfalls ahead on your small yes journey. Knowing when and how to say no is a skill you will need to develop in order to avoid these pitfalls.

## Pitfall #1: Not Enough Time

I do 60-70 coaching calls each month with business owners from around the world. The purpose of the calls is to help them identify their callings and then chart a meaningful course of action to get there. Once we know what we need to work on, the calls become more of an accountability measure to help the owners stay on track one small yes at a time.

Our calls cover many topics each week, but if there is one topic that comes up more than any other it is the challenge of TIME. It may be expressed in different ways, but all mentions of it point to the same sense of feeling overwhelmed with too many things to do and not enough time in the day to do them.

Does this sound familiar to you?

"If I only had a week with no interruptions."

"If I could just do my job instead of everybody else's work."

"There is not enough time in the day."

"It's all I can do to just keep going."

"I. Just. Don't. Have. Time."

If you are anything like the business owners I talk to each week, your lack of time is not because you have said yes too many times to your calling. Your lack of time is due to the fact that you have said yes to things that are not in line with the life you want to live.

The reasons people say yes to things they don't want to do are many:

- Sense of duty or obligation
- Guilt
- Desire to not disappoint others
- A blank space on the calendar

- Avoiding confrontation
- Avoiding real work
- A desire to please
- A need to impress

Every yes you say is an automatic no to something else–and that something else is likely being your family or working on your calling. It would be better to disappoint somebody for a few minutes by saying no now to something you don't want to do than to disappoint yourself or your family for a much longer time. Have the courage to say no to demands on your time so that you can say yes to the things you value most in life.

## Pitfall #2: Saying Yes in the Wrong Order

There are many challenges to saying yes to your calling. But once you've made the necessary space in your life to start following your calling, you are going to want to make sure that you are saying the right small yes at the right time. My dad said you need the right tool for the job; you also need the right yes for the task at hand.

Following your calling and building a life that makes a difference in the world is similar to building a house–all the elements are important, but they can't all be put in at the same time. When we were building our house, I had a tendency to get ahead of the contractor, having conversations and making deliveries the people on site weren't ready to receive. For example, I had no interest in wiring or the location of switch plates, but those Pottery Barn light fixtures? Well, I wanted their location marked before the house was framed. There were also times when the interest I showed in the building process came too late. To this day there's a pocket door where I wanted a window because I was too busy to tell the builder about my idea. There are also things in my house that I said yes to when I should've just said no. Every day I look at my bathroom and think to myself, "Does anybody really use a Jacuzzi tub? Who takes time to clean those vents?"

Just as there is a logical order to building a house, there is a logical order to saying yes as you follow your calling. Remember, the beauty of the one small yes journey is that you only have to say yes to the next thing, not the whole thing. Don't let your enthusiasm for the journey build things out of order or necessitate backtracking. Learn to say no so that you can build your calling in a sensible order. Rebuilding later is expensive–just ask my husband.

## Pitfall #3: Confusing Excellence With Unique Ability

According to Dan Sullivan, founder and creator of Strategic Coach, everyone spends their time in one of four areas:

- Incompetence
- Competence
- Excellence
- Unique Ability

Incompetence leads to frustration and feeling useless. Competence is marked by having the capacity to do something well, but never coming out ahead no matter how hard you try. Excellence results from natural skill that ends in achievement, but not necessarily enthusiasm. Unique ability is something that comes naturally just because you LOVE to do it. Unique ability is the place you could spend hours without ever remembering to take a break or to eat or drink.

Speaking of incompetence, an area of continual frustration for me is meal planning. I joke that I've never made a meal plan in my life because I prefer to choreograph my meals out of whatever is handy in the kitchen. The truth is that making plans for seven days of meals for a family of seven is simply too much detail work for this big picture gal. So instead I find creative ways to avoid going to the grocery store for days after my kids have started chanting, "Mo-om! There's no food in the house." The idea of planning food for a birthday party makes me break out in a cold sweat. Even if I make the list, I know I'm going to forget something important like the birthday cake itself. And Thanksgiving? Forget about it. I'm going to Grandma's house.

As for competence, most people would say that I am a competent dancer. I can hold my own in many styles of dance, but the reality is that no matter how much time, training or effort I put in, I'm not going to perform with New York City Ballet. My feet only arch so much and my legs only go so high. No amount of stretching is going to change the placement of my bones.

Excellence is a more curious topic. Dan asserts that most people end their careers at the excellence stage because they never discover their unique abilities. I was an excellent teacher. I could get more out of students emotionally and physically than most teachers I knew. But when I said yes to staying home with my kids and giving up teaching I found that I had an even greater, and unique, ability for business development and leadership.

Giving up teaching forced me to work on my business and become a leader. If I were no longer going to teach the bulk of the classes at my studio, I had to train and equip other people to do it. In doing so, I found out that I not only had a natural gift for training others, but I loved it as well. Now I use my unique ability to train not only my team, but also the leaders and teachers at our More Than Just Great Dancing® Affiliated Studios.

Incompetence and competence are easy to spot, but the difference between excellence and unique ability is harder to see. If you are going to fulfill your calling, you are going to need to practice saying yes to discovering and developing your unique abilities and saying no to spending so much time in your areas of incompetence, competence and as odd at is may seem, sometimes even saying no to your area of excellence.

## Pitfall #4: Self-Medicating

The term self-medicating was first observed in the *American Journal of Psychiatry* in 1985. It referred to a hypothesis that people with addictions will choose their drug based on how it makes them feel and the pain they are trying to ease. The term is typically associated with the abuse of alcohol, tobacco, over-the-counter medications and drugs.

But I would contend that self-medicating in other, more subtle and socially acceptable forms has become a way of life for many people in America. Consider the following:

- Food
- Television shows
- Social Media
- Netflix
- Magazines
- Email
- Texting
- Cell phones
- Shopping

Not one of the things on the list is bad in and of itself. But any activity you engage in to either make yourself feel better or to avoid dealing with difficult feelings or situations is a version of self-medicating–even if it is with socially acceptable activities.

People who have great callings will self-medicate for many reasons. These reasons include depression, fear, inadequacy, self-loathing, jealousy and a sense of being overwhelmed or ill-equipped. But one of the greatest reasons we self-medicate is to fight boredom. If you don't believe this is true, look at how many people pull out their phones in line at the grocery store or while waiting for a red light.

We have simply become a generation of people who are not comfortable with silence, being alone or being left out. Psychologists have come up with a term for the anxiety that is produced when you are convinced that something exciting is going on somewhere without you. It's called "FOMO," or the Fear Of Missing Out. If you aren't sure FOMO is real, take a cell phone from a teenager and watch them start to twitch.

If you are going to be able to say yes to the best things in your life, you are going to have to say no to self-medicating when you feel overwhelmed, anxious, bored or any of the other reasons that drive you to pick up your cell phone or binge watch Netflix. If you are going to make that mark on the world you were created to make; it is time to start saying no to self-medicating and replace it with an artful yes.

## Pitfall #5: Going it Alone

We discussed in several places so far the importance of saying yes to your priorities. Curious about this, I polled people at my live events asking them to rank how they were doing in prioritizing the following areas:

- Life partner
- Family
- Friends
- Money
- Career
- Health
- Leisure
- Spiritual Life

I surveyed groups for two consecutive years. The top scoring areas would vary from group to group, but interestingly, the bottom areas were always the same:

- Friends
- Leisure

At first, I was shocked. The people I polled were confident, capable people who were very clear on what kind of lives they wanted to live and the mark they intended to make on the world. They had beaten the challenges of yes and said yes to the daily disciplines required of their calling. They applied the tools they learned and made unconventional decisions as necessary. These people would be considered A-players in any room and they had the results to prove it.

But, apparently it's a lot easier to say yes to your calling than it is to say yes to yourself. Like many leaders, they were good at building businesses but not necessarily great at building meaningful relationships outside of the people they served. They found out very quickly that leadership, by its nature, can be lonely.

Dear reader, if you take nothing else from this book, please note this: Do not fall prey to the notion that you can go this road alone. I have tried that and it doesn't work. If you try to go it alone, even if it is just under the excuse of being too busy for friendships, you are going to end up burned out and resentful of your calling. Friends are a vital component of your ability to maintain a healthy relationship with your calling.

Tom Rath, the best-selling author of *Strengths Finder 2.0*, also wrote a book about friendship called *Vital Friends: The People You Can't Afford to Live Without*. According to Rath, we don't just need one friend; we need eight different kinds of friends for a healthy life:

- Builders to motivate you
- Champions to support you
- Collaborators to share your interests
- Companions who will always be there for you
- Connectors who help you get what you want
- Energizers to bring fun to your life
- Mind Openers to stretch your viewpoint
- Navigators to give you advice

Don't make the mistake of always putting your calling first and yourself last. Learn to say no to the lie that you are too busy for friends or that friendships are too messy to invest in. Practice saying no to the temptation to go it alone. You are going to need to lean on a variety of friends on the journey to fulfill your calling, so start building those relationships now.

## Pitfall #6: Measuring With the Wrong Stick

A few weeks ago I attended an event with a small group of friends. I had spent weeks preparing for the day and was ready to report on all I had accomplished since the last time we met. When I got there, one of the friends gave us all a t-shirt that said, "Don't measure yourself by what you have done, but by what you could've done with your ability."

Ouch.

Turns out I had been measuring with the wrong stick all along. I carried on with my presentation as planned, but I couldn't stop thinking about that quote on the t-shirt. On the plane ride home I mentally moved the stick to measure myself against what I could've done with my ability. I was disappointed with the answer.

Now I want to be really clear that my disappointment was not just about the fact that I could have done more. There is no doubt that I could have closed more sales and served more people and that I probably should have done so.

But what disappointed me most was not just thinking about what I could have DONE in that time, but who I could have BECOME. I had been so focused on saying one yes after another to my calling that I hadn't given the same daily attention to becoming the kind of person who would be able to carry the weight of the calling when I got there. I knew that where I was going with my calling would require more grace and grit than I had ever needed before. I took the quote from the t-shirt as a beautiful reminder that I needed to spend as much time working on who I was becoming as where I was going.

As I reflected on the quote and its meaning for my life, I remembered something another friend of mine had shared with me. Last I knew of him, he was the CEO of a large national company. When we ran into each other in an airport a few years later, he was working in a completely different industry. I asked him about his time as CEO and why he had walked away. He said he simply hadn't been ready to carry that weight.

The weight of your calling is likely bigger than your current capacity, too. You are going to have to say no to a lot of things to get ready for the task. No to time wasters. No to building things out of sequence just because you are more interested in some parts of building your calling than others. No to staying in your zone of excellence when you could be working in the zone of your unique ability. No to self-medicating in order to avoid hard work or difficult circumstances. And most importantly, even needing to say no to your calling on occasion to take time to work on yourself.

The real art of yes is knowing when to say no.

# Chapter 8

# My Wish for You

*I*t's time to paint a picture of what your life will be like when you follow your calling one small yes at a time. Go on, paint that picture in bright vivid colors! I believe that what God has planned for you and your life is more than you could possibly ask for or imagine.

You have been called to make a mark on the world that only you can make. You will be tempted at times to believe that you are not equal to the task, but you must remember: You. Are. Enough. You have been equipped with everything you need to do what you have been created to do. You just need to keep moving forward, one small yes at a time.

My wish for you until we meet again is that you would always know who you are and what you are called to do. Because who you are is as important to your calling as saying yes. Your identity is central to your calling even though what you do may change with time. Your personality will influence how you approach your calling–sometimes for better and sometimes for worse–so plan for it because the journey ahead is going to be a long one.

I want you to be able to block the distractions that will undoubtedly challenge your ability to continue saying yes to what you know you are called to do. Opportun-itis will surely come knocking if it hasn't already, and the doubters default is never far behind. Don't despise small beginnings; everybody starts somewhere.

Dream big blue-sky ideas, but develop the discipline of routines so that you aren't left to choose between distraction-actions and the real work of following your calling. Remember that while knowledge is good, it is not enough. You must plan the work and then work the plan. Take time to count the cost before you commit to the next yes. It just might cost you more than you are willing to pay.

Remember that among all of the good yes choices available to you, there will always be one best choice. Your job is to find it. Carry this quote with you as you make decisions about how to spend your limited time and resources:

"Not all GOOD things are GREAT things;
not all GREAT things are GOD things;
and not all GOD things are RIGHT NOW things."
**—Misty Lown**

Always make the best yes choice that you can and you will not be disappointed.

Life is hard. It's also daily, so develop concrete strategies that will help you continue to say you saying yes to your calling, even when you are tired or discouraged. Eat the live frog first each morning and lean on your mentors and motivators to push you when your push is gone. Know that there is a time to put on the brakes and a time to accelerate. Taking a rest doesn't mean you've given up on your calling, it means you are human. Remember, on average we make 35,000 decisions each day. That means you will have 35,000 opportunities to say yes to your calling today. If you miss one, grab the next one you can.

I pray that you will lower your expectations and understand that it is not possible to please everyone all the time. Grab hold of that truth early and well because no calling is worth losing your mind or your family. Get comfortable being off balance because you will be, a lot. And for the love of all things shiny, find a string for your kite–whether that person is a friend, spouse or co-worker. Kites without strings get stuck in trees, and how can you pursue your calling if you're stuck in a tree? Seriously. Get yourself a string.

Commit today to stop picking up socks and start moving rocks. Nobody ever changed the world with a fistful of socks, now did they? Have the courage to prune your life. So take a look at your calendar and your checkbook. They tell more about what you value than anything else. Start there and then prune out the deadwood to make room for new growth.

I wish for you a strong measure of the grace and grit required to make the unconventional decisions you need to make as you travel toward your calling. You might just be a square peg in a round hole someday, so get comfortable being misunderstood. It's nobody's journey but yours anyway.

Remember the fleeting nature of time. Let it squeeze your heart to slow down for times that matter and speed up for things you don't want to miss. And never apologize for taking time for your kids or to make memories with your parents. You only get to spend that time once.

When you get overwhelmed thinking of how big your calling is, remember that even the smallest yes in your weakest moment is all you need to keep going. There is a fight going on inside of you every day. Feed the good wolf. Develop a yes mindset and don't forget to look back to celebrate just how far you've come.

Most importantly, remember that the real art of yes is knowing when to say no. Don't let people and distractions steal your time. It's the most precious resource you have, so spend it doing things that matter–things that you have a unique ability to do. Don't numb yourself to difficult situations. Be OK being alone, but don't forget your friends. You'll need them on this journey.

Remember that picture I just asked you to paint? The one where you vividly imagine what your life will look like when you follow your calling? You are on your way and you will get there.

One small yes at a time.

# Acknowledgements

*One Small Yes* would not have been possible without the support of the following people. I am deeply thankful for your help and encouragement. The impact you have had on my life, and the lives of others through this work, cannot be measured with words.

Deak Swanson, my hero, you said the very first YES when you built a dance studio for me on a handshake 20 years ago. There is not a day that goes by that I don't remember your willingness to take a chance on the dreams of a kid from the North Side and I am committed to paying your kindness forward. I love that you call me your daughter and I hope to make you proud in the next 20 years as well!

Sandy Averill, my mom, you taught me how to care for people and put the needs of others before my own. You are the best listener and cheerleader a daughter could ask for. You picked me up every time I fell down and set me back in the race. Every success I have, I share with you.

Paul Averill, my dad, there is nothing that you can't figure out. My favorite memories of childhood are of building things with you. I'm still building like you taught me, but now I build businesses. I am so proud to be your daughter and my favorite hangout is still your garage.

Karen Lown, my mother-in-law, you have taught me so much about living life to the fullest. I am blessed beyond measure to have a mother-in-law who takes such an active interest in the lives of our kids. You help me to follow my calling every day. Thank you!

Alana Hess, my sister, or should I say "Seesta", you have gone from the little one who followed me around to the one who leads my businesses. You are an amazing leader, wife and mother. I'm very proud of you and I can't wait to see what we will build in the future!

Katie and Emily Lown, my sisters-in-law by marriage, friends by choice: Katie, you inspire me to always keep God in first place. Emily you spent two weeks helping me pack and make a Popsicle stick tracking system because I couldn't afford software at the time. Thank you!

Shayna Stellflue, my friend, there is no part of this journey that would have been complete without you. You have worked steadily by my side just as long and as hard as I have. Thank you for always believing in me when I say, "So…I have an idea!" Twenty years into this and we are just getting started!

Liz Camacho, my protégé, you once told me that you were going to pay forward the mentoring I gave you as a teenager and you most certainly have. Last month alone more than 1 million people were inspired by what you built with MoreThanDancers.com. You inspire me as well!

Megan McCluskey, my creative director, you closed your business to help me build mine. I will never forget that! You have the unique ability to turn everything that I see in my mind into something real. Thank you for turning my dreams into reality.

Annette Mikat, my advisor, you are the great connector. You connect ideas and people to transform our community. You have helped me to navigate difficult waters and chart a course for where I want to go. You have a real gift, thank you for sharing it with me!

Kris Nandory, Sandy Averill, Toni Key, Julie Vannucchi, Tiffany Fischer, Kylie Williams, Katie Reischl and Shayna Stellflue, the Misty's Dance Unlimited leadership team. The studio is the foundation of the More Than Just Great Dancing® movement worldwide because of the way you and all of our amazing TEACHERS care for students and families each day. Our community is blessed because you teach our students to share their gifts and talents with others.

MDU dance families and students, you believed in the More Than Just Great Dancing® studio environment long before it was a logo or anything to talk about. Your enthusiasm and authentic interest in seeing kids develop from the inside out through the arts motivates me every day to be a better leader and teacher.

Janelle Perry, Krisa Roggensack, Liz Camacho, Julie Vannucchi, Toni Key, Megan McCluskey, Alana Hess, Pat Mundsack, Michelle Malone, Terri Tobin and Denise Meyer, the More Than Just Great Dancing® leadership team and contributors, you have put heart and soul into this startup company and I cannot thank you enough! You understand the significance of equipping other studio owners to follow *their* callings and you have become world changers in the process.

MTJGD studio owners, aka "The Tribe," you are the heart and soul of the More Than Just Great Dancing® movement. I would never be able to serve 60,000 students on my own, but together we do just that each week! You are the true leaders in the industry–shaping the next generation of dancers and world changers. My gratitude for you runs deep.

Marvin Wanders, my first mentor in business, you have given me so many opportunities to grow and learn. I will be forever thankful for you and your family. The day you gave me a subscription to SUCCESS magazine changed my life, and I'm looking forward to our next project together.

Darren and Georgia Hardy, my mentors and friends, the entire More Than Just Great Dancing® concept was birthed at your High Performance Forum. And every event since that time has continued to shape what we do–from training owners to exposing students to your leadership principles. You set out to "influence influencers" and you certainly have!

Brad Pedersen, my peak performance partner, you are a compass for my life, marriage, parenting and business. Your wisdom and generosity never cease to amaze me, and I am working hard to follow your example every step of the way.

Dave Liniger, my mentor and friend, I can't tell if the Lowns adopted the Linigers or if the Linigers adopted the Lowns! Either way we can't imagine life without you, Gail and Max. The kids talk about you pretty much every day and I am so grateful to call you my mentor. I am still working on my "Book of Dave" with all the lessons I've been accumulating.

Marc Sparks, Paul Niccum and Cody Foster and my other Elite colleagues, what you have built in your businesses and how you lead your people inspires me everyday to play better, think bigger and give more generously. Thank you for taking my calls and visits–I've taken many notes!

Dave Skogen, my role model and friend, I didn't know you personally when I opened my dance studio two decades ago, but I told people that I was going to be the "Festival Foods of dance" because your stores were brighter, cleaner and friendlier than the others and gave so much to the community. That is still my goal and I can't believe I get to work with you now to bring servant leadership to area students.

Michelle Brogan, my boss and friend, I brought my students to Dance Revolution 13 years ago to give them a life-changing experience in dance and faith. My own life has been changed every bit as much as theirs. Your visionary leadership has paved the way for so many and I love being on your team!

Tighe King, my first national supporter, you stepped up to be the very first title sponsor of Studio Owner University® and you've been with us ever since. You have outfitted the dance industry for 47 years and you are still the innovator.

John and Marica Splinter, our first pastors as a couple, you showed us what community and faith could look like through Point of Grace. I hope to create that same kind of environment in my home and businesses. Grace wins every time!

Diane Gebhart, my high school coach, you saw something in me when I didn't see it in myself. I still have the *Oh, The Places You'll Go* book that you gave me for graduation, and I read to my children. The story is timeless!

Sally Stinson and Phil Addis, my Oktoberfest team: Sally, you encouraged me to try one more time when I didn't become Miss La Crosse Oktoberfest the first time I tried. The second time I tried, I won and Deak Swanson was my Festmaster. And as they say, the rest is history. Phil you taught me how to interview and then set up my first LLC—two things I still use to this day. Thank you!

Terry Erickson, my first boss, you gave me my first job as a dance teacher at the Boys & Girls Club. Twenty-five years later we have kids from the Club come and take class every week at the studio. What a full circle!

Janell Larson, my first company director, you showed me what empowering another person to carry out our mission could look like. You work paved the road for the programs we run today, and you still give to our students generously. Thank you!

Amoreena Clark, Carmen Larson, Angela Kruger, Dawn Duellman, Shannon Krautkramer and Asha Bianca, the girlfriends, you all hold a special place in my life for different reasons. Thank you for creating a space for me to just be me. Every girl should have a group of friends like you.

Angela Lauria and Cynthia Kane, my publisher and editor, you are the dream team! I have talked about writing a book for years, but you made the actual writing process possible. Difference Press is the perfect name for what you do–you help people make a difference with a book.

# About the Author

Misty Lown is the founder, president and energizing force behind More Than Just Great Dancing®, a licensed dance studio affiliation program that has a positive influence on more than 60,000 dance students around the globe each week. She is also the founder of MoreThanDancers.com, an online lifestyle magazine for young people that has more than 200,000 visitors each month.

Her dance studio, Misty's Dance Unlimited, founded in 1998 and named a "Top 50 Studios in the Nation" by Dance Spirit Magazine, has provided more than $250,000 in scholarships for dancers and other community initiatives. Misty has been a speaker at the PULSE Teachers Convention, Hollywood Connection, Dance Teacher Web, Dance Teacher Summit, and the DanceLife Conference. She has also been the keynote speaker for the Australian Teachers of Dancing Convention. Misty is on the staff of Dance Revolution Convention, a faith-based dance convention, and has authored more than 40 industry articles.

She is a sought-after speaker and recently shared her business methods as a guest blogger on SUCCESS.com and as a speaker at IF:Gathering Local and the U.S. Army Garrison Women's Equality Day. She has been recognized as "Teacher of the Year" by Eclipse, "Outstanding Businesswoman of the Year" by YWCA La Crosse and awarded the "Pope John XXIII Award for Distinguished Service" by Viterbo University and the "Philanthropy Award" from the Southwest Chapter of the American Red Cross of Wisconsin.

Misty is an entrepreneur at heart. In addition to her dance studio and licensing program, she owns a dancewear store, a dance competition and a self-storage business. Misty's favorite part of the day is spending time with her husband and five beautiful children.

# Thank You

## How to Keep Saying YES

It's time to start building the life of significance you were made to live! If you are going to follow your calling, it's important that you have access to a community that will help you keep saying yes long after you've finished this book. Even though you have finished the *One Small Yes* book, you are just getting started on your journey. I've prepared some special opportunities and resources for you to help you stay plugged in so that you can keep saying yes to *your* calling. Let's start!

## Studio Owners

Visit MoreThanJustGreatDancing.com for free, up-to-date dance studio business content. You will have access to videos, articles, blogs and downloads about building a studio business that makes a difference. You can also sign up for a free weekly motivator called the "Misty Minute" and more!

Join me at my annual Studio Owner University® where I will teach you the 9 Essential Building Blocks of a successful dance studio business along with the most current information regarding marketing, technology, business best practices and so much more! It's like going back to college to learn the business side of the dance studio. First time attendees can deduct 50 percent off the registration with the following code: ONESMALLYES. Details are available at StudioOwnerUniversity.com.

## Dancers

Visit MoreThanDancers.com for free resources including helpful and encouraging articles, profiles and videos about dance, life, beauty, school and much more! Take fun quizzes and find information about our live event. Sign up for a free account to receive 10 percent off your first order from the MoreThanDancers.com store.

## Entrepreneurs, Students and Leaders

Find more ideas for developing a strategy to accomplish your daily routine by downloading a free copy of the One Small Yes Daily Routine worksheet at OneSmallYes.com. You can also sign up for a free weekly motivator called the "Misty Minute" and much more!

## Keynote Speaking & Consulting

For information about hiring Misty to give a keynote address for your next event or to provide consulting for your corporation or association, please visit MistyLown.com.

www.TheMorganJamesSpeakersGroup.com

We connect Morgan James published authors with live and online events and audiences whom will benefit from their expertise.

Morgan James
Speakers Group

Morgan James makes all of our titles available
through the Library for All Charity Organizations.

www.LibraryForAll.org

CPSIA information can be obtained
at www.ICGtesting.com
Printed in the USA
LVOW03s1951270717
542866LV00005B/842/P